מסורה

ArtScroll Mesorah Series®

Expositions on Jewish liturgy and thought

Rabbi Nosson Scherman
Rabbi Meir Zlotowitz
General Editors

Published by

Mesorah Publications, ltd

ARTSCROLL
youth haggadah

New simplified translation and comments by
Rabbis Nosson and Yitzchok Zev Scherman

Full-color Illustrations by
Yosef Dershowitz and Dovid Sears

Co-edited by
Rabbis Meir Zlotowitz and Avie Gold

Designed by
Rabbi Sheah Brander

This Haggadah is dedicated
to the memory of

Rabbi Meir Levi ז"ל

כ"ד חשון תשכ"ט

Rebbetzin Shoshana Levi ע"ה

י"ג כסלו תשל"ט

*Pioneers and molders of girls' chinuch in America,
they founded, led, taught — and set sterling personal examples —
in the Bais Yaakov of Brownsville, East New York, and Crown Heights.*

*By creating Camp Hedvah, they showed how much
an intelligently crafted summer can enrich a girl's life.*

*Their tradition lives on in Bais Yaakov d'Rav Meir and Camp Hedvah
where their legacy of והגדת לבנך continues to thrive in their children.*

תנצב"ה

FIRST EDITION
Nine Impressions:
March 1987 . . . January 1998

Published and Distributed by
MESORAH PUBLICATIONS, Ltd.
4401 Second Avenue
Brooklyn, New York 11232

Distributed in Europe by
J. LEHMANN HEBREW BOOKSELLERS
20 Cambridge Terrace / Gateshead, Tyne and Wear / England NE8 1RP

Distributed in Israel by
SIFRIATI / A. GITLER — BOOKS
10 Hashomer Street / Bnei Brak 51361

Distributed in Australia & New Zealand by
GOLDS BOOK & GIFT CO.
36 William Street / Balaclava 3183 / Vic., Australia

Distributed in South Africa by
KOLLEL BOOKSHOP
Shop 8A Norwood Hypermarket / Norwood 2196 / Johannesburg, South Africa

ARTSCROLL MESORAH SERIES ®
YOUTH HAGGADAH
© *Copyright 1987, 1994, by* MESORAH PUBLICATIONS, Ltd. / 4401 Second Avenue / Brooklyn, N.Y. 11232 / (718) 921-9000

ISBN: 0-89906-232-6 (hard cover)
ISBN: 0-89906-233-4 (paperback)

Typography by CompuScribe at ArtScroll Studios, Ltd.
4401 Second Avenue / Brooklyn, N.Y. 11232 / (718) 921-9000

The Seder / Still Going Free

Pesach has a special place in Jewish life. On Pesach we became free. On Pesach we became a nation. On Pesach God made us His Own people. We say about many of our *mitzvos* that they remind us of the time when God took us out of Egypt. The Torah commands us to remember every day in our morning and evening prayers that God saved us from Egypt.

There is a special *mitzvah* at the Seder for children and parents to speak to each other about the miracles of this day. Children should ask questions about the *mitzvos* and the miracles of Pesach, and their parents should explain to them. When the littlest member of the household stands before his father or grandfather and tries to go through the *Mah Nishtanah* — while everyone else smiles and helps with the next word — that child is doing what the young Rambam, the young Rabbi Yehudah Hanassi and the young King Solomon did. And when the leader of the *Seder* says, "You have asked very well, my child, and now I will answer you," and then he begins to read the *Haggadah* and explain that we were once slaves, and if God had not saved us we would *still* be slaves — he is giving the same answer that Jewish parents have given all the way back to the time of Moses.

And in the *Haggadah* we say that every Jew should feel as if God had saved *us* — not just our forefathers — from Egypt. That is the key to the *Seder*. This night is a new beginning for us. Can we imagine how excited the Jewish people must have been at their first *Seder* in Egypt, knowing that soon they would go free to receive the Torah and enter *Eretz Yisrael*? That is how excited we should feel at our *Seder*. It is as if God were doing all those miracles for us — tonight! On the first Pesach we stopped being slaves. What about today? From what can we go free on *this* Pesach? In some countries, our brothers and sisters do not have real freedom. Even those of us in free lands may have problems that make it hard for us to serve God the way we would like to. Some of us are so busy with all sorts of things that we don't even understand *how* to serve God or what our special responsibilities are as Jews! Isn't that a lot like slavery? Whenever a person thinks that he *must* do certain things or that he is not free to do other things, that is a kind of slavery.

At the *Seder*, we remember that if we truly want to be free to serve God, and if He is ready to accept us, there is no force in the World that can stand in His way. Rivers can turn to blood, wild animals can appear from nowhere, firstborn people can suddenly die, and seas can split — no miracle is too hard for God. If God could do it in the year 2448 after Creation, when our forefathers left Egypt, He can do it today. If we truly feel and believe that — it is as if we ourselves were being freed from Egypt.

❈ ❈ ❈

This new *Haggadah* is special, and not just because it has full-color illustrations and is so beautiful. The reason we produced it is because we wanted everyone, young and old, to understand the *Haggadah* better than ever before — some people, perhaps for the first time. The new translation explains everything clearly. The comments on most pages are there so that even youngsters will be able to add something to the *Seder*.

The Torah wants the *Seder* to be a partnership of all the generations, because all of us went free — and are still going free — tonight. If, indeed, this *Haggadah* can help people make their *Seder* a bit better than it was, we will be grateful. Let us all hope and pray that this year, this Pesach, this *Seder* will bring the fulfillment of the prophecy: "כִּימֵי צֵאתְךָ מֵאֶרֶץ מִצְרָיִם אַרְאֶנּוּ נִפְלָאוֹת", *As in the days when you left Egypt, I will show him miracles*" (Micah 7:15), with the coming of *Mashiach*, speedily in our days.

בְּדִיקַת חָמֵץ
The Search for Chametz

At nightfall of the evening before the first *Seder,* every home and business must be searched thoroughly for *chametz.* The search should be made by candlelight. From the time the blessing is recited until the end of the search, those doing it should not speak — except to give instructions or ask questions about the search. In most families, it is customary to spread ten pieces of *chametz* around the house, so that the searchers will have something to look for. [If the first *Seder* is on Saturday night, the search is made on Thursday night.]

We bless You, HASHEM our God, King of the whole world, Who has made us holy with His commandments, and commanded us about the removal of Chametz.

בָּרוּךְ אַתָּה יהוה אֱלֹהֵינוּ מֶלֶךְ הָעוֹלָם, אֲשֶׁר קִדְּשָׁנוּ בְּמִצְוֹתָיו, וְצִוָּנוּ עַל בִּעוּר חָמֵץ.

After the search, the *chametz* is wrapped and put away to be burned the next morning. The following declaration is made. Since the declaration must be understood by the person saying it, someone who does not understand the text should recite it in English or any other language he understands. The declaration does not refer to *chametz* that has been set aside to be eaten, sold, or used before the deadline on the next morning.

Any Chametz that is in my possession, which I did not see and remove, and which I do not know about, shall be as if it does not exist and shall become ownerless, like the dust of the earth.

כָּל חֲמִירָא וַחֲמִיעָא דְּאִכָּא בִרְשׁוּתִי, דְּלָא חֲמִתֵּהּ וּדְלָא בְעַרְתֵּהּ וּדְלָא יָדַעְנָא לֵהּ, לִבָּטֵל וְלֶהֱוֵי הֶפְקֵר כְּעַפְרָא דְאַרְעָא.

בְּעוּר חָמֵץ
Burning the Chametz

The *chametz* that has been found in the search, along with *chametz* left over from breakfast, is burned in the morning. The following declaration is made after the *chametz* is burned. It refers to all *chametz* without exception. [When Pesach begins on Saturday night, this declaration is made on Saturday morning, after the meal. Any *chametz* remaining from the Saturday morning meal, should be flushed down the drain before the declaration is made.] Since the declaration must be understood by the person saying it, someone who does not understand that text should recite it in English or any other language he understands.

Any Chametz that is in my possession, whether I did or did not recognize it, whether I did or did not see it, whether I did or did not remove it, shall be as if it does not exist and shall become ownerless, like the dust of the earth.

כָּל חֲמִירָא וַחֲמִיעָא דְּאִכָּא בִרְשׁוּתִי, דַּחֲזִתֵּהּ וּדְלָא חֲזִתֵּהּ, דַּחֲמִתֵּהּ וּדְלָא חֲמִתֵּהּ, דְּבִעַרְתֵּהּ וּדְלָא בְעַרְתֵּהּ, לִבָּטֵל וְלֶהֱוֵי הֶפְקֵר כְּעַפְרָא דְאַרְעָא.

עֵרוּב תַּבְשִׁילִין
Eruv Tavshilin

The following blessing and declaration are recited when the first days of Pesach fall on Thursday and Friday. Ordinarily it is forbidden to prepare food on *Yom Tov* for the next day, even if it is the Sabbath. However, if someone began his Sabbath food preparations before *Yom Tov,* it is permitted to continue them on *Yom Tov.* This is the reason for *Eruv Tavshilin:* we take a matzah and a cooked food (egg, fish, or meat) on the afternoon before *Yom Tov,* set them aside to be eaten on the Sabbath, and recite the following.

We bless You, HASHEM our God, King of the whole world, Who made us holy with His commandments, and commanded us concerning the commandment of Eruv.

בָּרוּךְ אַתָּה יהוה אֱלֹהֵינוּ מֶלֶךְ הָעוֹלָם, אֲשֶׁר קִדְּשָׁנוּ בְּמִצְוֹתָיו, וְצִוָּנוּ עַל מִצְוַת עֵרוּב.

Since the following declaration must be understood by the person saying it, someone who does not understand the text should recite it in English or any other language that he understands.

Through this Eruv may we be permitted to bake, cook, fry, insulate, kindle flame, prepare for, and do anything necessary on the festival for the sake of the Sabbath (for ourselves and for all Jews who live in this city).

בְּהָדֵין עֵרוּבָא יְהֵא שָׁרֵא לָנָא לַאֲפוּיֵי וּלְבַשּׁוּלֵי וּלְאַצְלוּיֵי וּלְאַטְמוּנֵי וּלְאַדְלוּקֵי שְׁרָגָא וּלְתַקָּנָא וּלְמֶעְבַּד כָּל צָרְכָּנָא, מִיּוֹמָא טָבָא לְשַׁבַּתָּא (לָנָא וּלְכָל יִשְׂרָאֵל הַדָּרִים בָּעִיר הַזֹּאת).

Lighting the Candles — הַדְלָקַת הַנֵּרוֹת

The candles are lit and the following blessings are recited.
[When Pesach falls on the Sabbath, the words in brackets are added.]

We bless You, HASHEM our God, King of the whole world, Who has made us holy with His commandments and commanded us to kindle the flame of the [Shabbos and the] Yom Tov.

בָּרוּךְ אַתָּה יהוה אֱלֹהֵינוּ מֶלֶךְ הָעוֹלָם, אֲשֶׁר קִדְּשָׁנוּ בְּמִצְוֹתָיו, וְצִוָּנוּ לְהַדְלִיק נֵר שֶׁל [שַׁבָּת וְשֶׁל] יוֹם טוֹב.

We bless You, HASHEM our God, King of the whole world, for keeping us alive, taking care of us, and bringing us to this season.

בָּרוּךְ אַתָּה יהוה אֱלֹהֵינוּ מֶלֶךְ הָעוֹלָם, שֶׁהֶחֱיָנוּ וְקִיְּמָנוּ וְהִגִּיעָנוּ לַזְּמַן הַזֶּה.

≈{ The Seder Plate — הַקְּעָרָה }≈

Everything that will be needed for the *Seder* should be prepared in advance. The *Seder* should begin as soon as possible after synagogue services have ended. However, it should not begin before night fall.

Matzah, bitter vegetables and several other foods are placed on the קְעָרָה or *Seder* plate. The picture on the next page shows how they are arranged in front of the father (or other person leading the *Seder*).

זְרוֹעַ, **Z'ro'a** [roasted bone] and בֵּיצָה, **Beitzah** [roasted egg] — On the afternoon before the Pesach holiday,

two offerings would be brought in the *Bais Hamikdash* [Holy Temple] in Jerusalem. One was the *Pesach* offering, the other was the *Chagigah* offering. Their meat was roasted and was eaten at the *Seder* feast.

To remind us of these two offerings we place a roasted bone (with some meat on it) and a roasted egg on the *Seder* plate. However, the meat on the roasted bone (or any other roasted meat) may not be eaten at the *Seder*. If roast meat were eaten at the *Seder* it would seem as if we are eating the meat of the offerings, something we may do only when the *Bais Hamikdash* is standing.

The word *z'ro'a* means shankbone or arm. Although any meaty bone may be used, we call it *z'ro'a* to hint at the זְרוֹעַ נְטוּיָה, outstretched "arm," with which God took us out of Egypt.

The egg, a traditional symbol of mourning, is used instead of a second piece of meat as a sign of our mourning at the loss of the *Bais Hamikdash,* may it be rebuilt soon, in our lifetime.

מָרוֹר, **Marror** and חֲזֶרֶת, **Chazeres** [two kinds of bitter vegetables] — We eat bitter vegetables twice during the

Seder: once by themselves as MARROR; the second time with matzah as KORECH. Each time a portion equal in volume to half an egg should be eaten.

Two kinds of bitter vegetables are placed on the *Seder* plate — most people use romaine lettuce (whole leaves or stalks) and raw horseradish (whole or grated). Either or both may be used for the MARROR and KORECH during the *Seder.*

חֲרוֹסֶת, **Charoses** — The *marror* is dipped into *charoses,* a mixture of grated apples, nuts, other fruits, cinnamon and other spices, and red wine. *Charoses* looks and feels like mortar and reminds us of the hard work that the Jewish slaves had to do in Egypt.

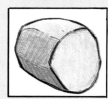

כַּרְפַּס, **Karpas** — A vegetable other than *marror* — most people use celery, parsley or boiled potato — is dipped into salt water and eaten. The vegetable, called *karpas,* is placed on the *Seder* plate. The salt water, a symbol of the sweat and tears of the slaves, is not placed on the plate. It should be prepared beforehand and placed near the *Seder* plate.

מַצָּה, **Matzah** — Three whole matzos are placed one above the other separated by a cloth or napkin. *Matzah*

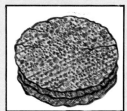

is eaten at least three times during the *Seder:* once by itself as MATZAH; the second time with *marror* as KORECH; the third time by itself as TZAFUN (the *Afikoman*). Each time a portion equal in volume to half an egg should be eaten. It is necessary to have an extra supply of matzah at hand in order to be sure that each person receives a full portion.

Although any matzah prepared especially for Pesach may be eaten during the rest of the meal, these three portions must be of *matzah sh'murah,* a special matzah made from wheat that was designated for the *mitzvah* of matzah and was guarded against moisture from the moment it was cut from the field.

אַרְבָּעָה כּוֹסוֹת, **Four Cups of Wine** — At four points during the *Seder* [at the end of the KADDESH, MAGGID,

BARECH and HALLEL sections of the *Seder*], each person drinks a cup of wine. According to a verse in *Mishlei* (Proverbs), red wine is preferable. The cup should be large enough to hold a *reviis* of wine. Opinions about the modern equivalent of a *reviis* range from three to more than five fluid ounces.

Although it is preferable to drink the entire cup each time, one who cannot do so may fulfill the *mitzvah* by drinking more than half the cup.

סִימָנֵי הַסֵדֶר

THE ORDER OF THE SEDER

Wash the hands before eating karpas.

Recite the Kiddush.

Break the middle matzah.

Eat a vegetable dipped in salt water.

Wash the hands before eating matzah.

Tell the Pesach story.

מָרוֹר

MARROR

Eat the bitter herbs.

מוֹצִיא מַצָּה

MOTZI MATZAH

Eat the matzah.

שֻׁלְחָן עוֹרֵךְ

SHULCHAN ORECH

Eat the festive meal.

כּוֹרֵךְ

KORECH

Eat a sandwich of matzah and *marror.*

בָּרֵךְ

BARECH

Recite *Bircas Hamazon* (Grace after Meals).

צָפוּן

TZAFUN

Eat the *Afikoman.*

נִרְצָה

NIRTZAH

Pray that God accepts our *mitzvah.*

הַלֵּל

HALLEL

Recite psalms of praise.

The *Seder* should start as soon as possible after the synagogue services, but not before nightfall.

קַדֵּשׁ

KADDESH

THE FIRST CUP IS FILLED.

At the *Seder* we should act in a way that shows freedom and majesty —
therefore, each person's cup should be filled by someone else.

The father (or whoever leads the *Seder*) recites *Kiddush*. In some families, all others listen and respond אָמֵן, *Amen*.
In other families, all recite *Kiddush* quietly along with the father, or one at a time after the father.

Hold up the cup in the right hand while reciting *Kiddush*.

On Friday night begin *Kiddush* with this paragraph:

And it was evening and it was morning — [the end of]
The sixth day.

And the heaven, the earth, and everything in them were finished. So on the seventh day, God stopped His work that He had been doing; and He rested on the seventh day from all His work that He had been doing. God blessed the seventh day and made it holy (by giving us special *Shabbos mitzvos*) because on that day God rested from all His work that God had created, so that it would be productive.

Quietly—וַיְהִי עֶרֶב וַיְהִי בֹקֶר —
Aloud—יוֹם הַשִּׁשִּׁי.

וַיְכֻלּוּ הַשָּׁמַיִם וְהָאָרֶץ וְכָל צְבָאָם. וַיְכַל אֱלֹהִים בַּיּוֹם הַשְּׁבִיעִי מְלַאכְתּוֹ אֲשֶׁר עָשָׂה, וַיִּשְׁבֹּת בַּיּוֹם הַשְּׁבִיעִי מִכָּל מְלַאכְתּוֹ אֲשֶׁר עָשָׂה. וַיְבָרֶךְ אֱלֹהִים אֶת יוֹם הַשְּׁבִיעִי וַיְקַדֵּשׁ אֹתוֹ, כִּי בוֹ שָׁבַת מִכָּל מְלַאכְתּוֹ אֲשֶׁר בָּרָא אֱלֹהִים לַעֲשׂוֹת.

On all nights other than Friday night, begin *Kiddush* here:

With your permission.

We bless You, HASHEM our God, King of the whole world, Who creates the fruit of the grapevine.

סַבְרִי מָרָנָן וְרַבָּנָן וְרַבּוֹתַי.
בָּרוּךְ אַתָּה יהוה אֱלֹהֵינוּ מֶלֶךְ הָעוֹלָם, בּוֹרֵא פְּרִי הַגָּפֶן.

(Others respond: אָמֵן, *Amen)*

e bless You, HASHEM our God, King of the whole world, because You chose us as Your special nation from

בָּרוּךְ אַתָּה יהוה אֱלֹהֵינוּ מֶלֶךְ הָעוֹלָם, אֲשֶׁר בָּחַר בָּנוּ מִכָּל

all the other nations in the world and You made us higher than those who speak any other language, and made us holy by giving us *mitzvos* to do. To show how much You love us, HASHEM our God, You gave us [*Shabbosos* for rest and] special times for gladness, Festivals and seasons for rejoicing, this day of [*Shabbos* and this day of] the Festival of Matzos, the time when we went free [with love], a holy day that is a reminder that You took us out of Egypt. For You chose us and made us holier than all the nations, and You gave us [*Shabbos* and] Your special holy days [with love and favor], with gladness and with joy to pass on to our children. We bless You, HASHEM, because You gave holiness to [*Shabbos*], the Jewish people, and *Yom Tov*.

עָם, וְרוֹמְמָנוּ מִכָּל לָשׁוֹן, וְקִדְּשָׁנוּ בְּמִצְוֹתָיו. וַתִּתֶּן לָנוּ יהוה אֱלֹהֵינוּ בְּאַהֲבָה [שַׁבָּתוֹת לִמְנוּחָה וּ]מוֹעֲדִים לְשִׂמְחָה, חַגִּים וּזְמַנִּים לְשָׂשׂוֹן, אֶת יוֹם [הַשַּׁבָּת הַזֶּה וְאֶת יוֹם] חַג הַמַּצוֹת הַזֶּה, זְמַן חֵרוּתֵנוּ [בְּאַהֲבָה] מִקְרָא קֹדֶשׁ, זֵכֶר לִיצִיאַת מִצְרָיִם, כִּי בָנוּ בָחַרְתָּ וְאוֹתָנוּ קִדַּשְׁתָּ מִכָּל הָעַמִּים, [וְשַׁבָּת] וּמוֹעֲדֵי קָדְשֶׁךָ [בְּאַהֲבָה וּבְרָצוֹן] בְּשִׂמְחָה וּבְשָׂשׂוֹן הִנְחַלְתָּנוּ. בָּרוּךְ אַתָּה יהוה, מְקַדֵּשׁ [הַשַּׁבָּת וְ]יִשְׂרָאֵל וְהַזְּמַנִּים.

(Others respond: אָמֵן, *Amen*)

On Saturday night add the following two blessings.
During the first blessing, two candles should be held close together so that their flames touch each other.
Hold your fingers up to the flame and look at the reflected light on your fingernails.

e bless You, HASHEM our God, King of the whole world, Who creates the lights of the fire.

בָּרוּךְ אַתָּה יהוה אֱלֹהֵינוּ מֶלֶךְ הָעוֹלָם, בּוֹרֵא מְאוֹרֵי הָאֵשׁ.

(Others respond: אָמֵן, *Amen*)

e bless You, HASHEM our God, King of the whole world, because You separate holy things from things that are not holy; light from darkness; the Jewish people from the other nations, and *Shabbos* from the six working days. You separated the holiness of *Shabbos* from the holiness of *Yom Tov*, and You made *Shabbos* holier than the six working days. You made Your Jewish people separate and holy by giving them Your own holiness. We bless You, HASHEM, because You separate one kind of holiness from another.

בָּרוּךְ אַתָּה יהוה אֱלֹהֵינוּ מֶלֶךְ הָעוֹלָם, הַמַּבְדִּיל בֵּין קֹדֶשׁ לְחֹל, בֵּין אוֹר לְחֹשֶׁךְ, בֵּין יִשְׂרָאֵל לָעַמִּים, בֵּין יוֹם הַשְּׁבִיעִי לְשֵׁשֶׁת יְמֵי הַמַּעֲשֶׂה. בֵּין קְדֻשַּׁת שַׁבָּת לִקְדֻשַּׁת יוֹם טוֹב הִבְדַּלְתָּ, וְאֶת יוֹם הַשְּׁבִיעִי מִשֵּׁשֶׁת יְמֵי הַמַּעֲשֶׂה קִדַּשְׁתָּ, הִבְדַּלְתָּ וְקִדַּשְׁתָּ אֶת עַמְּךָ יִשְׂרָאֵל בִּקְדֻשָּׁתֶךָ. בָּרוּךְ אַתָּה יהוה, הַמַּבְדִּיל בֵּין קֹדֶשׁ לְקֹדֶשׁ.

(Others respond: אָמֵן, *Amen*)

On all nights *Kiddush* ends with this blessing:

We bless You, HASHEM our God, King of the whole world, for keeping us alive, taking care of us, and bringing us to this season.

בָּרוּךְ אַתָּה יהוה אֱלֹהֵינוּ מֶלֶךְ הָעוֹלָם, שֶׁהֶחֱיָנוּ וְקִיְּמָנוּ וְהִגִּיעָנוּ לַזְּמַן הַזֶּה.

(Others respond: אָמֵן, *Amen*)

Drink the wine immediately, while seated and reclining on the left side.

It is preferable to drink the entire cup, but at the very least, most of the cup.

URECHATZ

Wash your hands [by pouring water from a cup, twice on the right hand, then twice on the left] as if washing for matzah, but do not recite a blessing.

KARPAS

Take a small piece of *karpas* (a vegetable other than the *marror)* and dip it in salt-water.

The *karpas* is dipped to show majesty and freedom; paupers and slaves do not dip their vegetables.

Salt-water is used instead of fancy dressing to remind us of our salty tears and sweat when we were slaves in Egypt.

Recite the blessing (keeping in mind that the blessing also applies to the *marror* which will be eaten later).

We bless You, HASHEM our God, King of the whole world, Who creates fruit that grows from the ground.

בָּרוּךְ אַתָּה יהוה אֱלֹהֵינוּ מֶלֶךְ הָעוֹלָם, בּוֹרֵא פְּרִי הָאֲדָמָה.

Eat the vegetable. It is not necessary to recline while eating *karpas,* but some people do recline

YACHATZ

We are about to tell the story of our slavery in Egypt and how God made us free. Poor slaves never have enough to eat, so they put something away for the next meal — because there may be nothing to eat later! We break the matzah now and put some away for later to remind ourselves of the slavery.

The father breaks the middle matzah in two and wraps the larger part to use later as the *Afikoman.*

Some people put the *Afikoman* on their shoulder for a few moments and say, בְּבֶהָלוּ יָצָאנוּ מִמִּצְרַיִם, *We left Egypt in a hurry,* to remind us that the Jews carried the matzos on their shoulders when they left Egypt.

The next part of the *Haggadah* tells the story of how God saved us from slavery in Egypt. The father should explain the story so that everyone can understand.

The father holds up the broken middle matzah as he recites the next paragraph.

This is the plain, poor bread

הָא לַחְמָא עַנְיָא

that our parents ate in the land of Egypt. Whoever is hungry, come eat with us. Whoever needs a place to stay, come make Pesach with us. This year we are here — next year may we be in *Eretz Yisrael*. This year we are not free — next year may we be free to serve God perfectly!

דִּי אֲכָלוּ אַבְהָתָנָא בְּאַרְעָא דְמִצְרָיִם. כָּל דִּכְפִין יֵיתֵי וְיֵכוֹל, כָּל דִּצְרִיךְ יֵיתֵי וְיִפְסַח. הָשַׁתָּא הָכָא, לְשָׁנָה הַבָּאָה בְּאַרְעָא דְיִשְׂרָאֵל. הָשַׁתָּא עַבְדֵי, לְשָׁנָה הַבָּאָה בְּנֵי חוֹרִין.

The broken matzah is put back between the two whole matzos.

הָא לַחְמָא עַנְיָא — This is the plain, poor bread.

Once a very poor man suddenly became rich. Every year, on the anniversary of the day he became wealthy, he would make a party for his whole family. At the party, he would wear his shabby, old clothes to remind everybody of how poor he used to be.

Then his business went bad and he lost all his money. After a while he even had to sell all his good clothes. One morning, the only things he had to wear were his shabby, old clothes. When his children saw him, they jumped up and down in excitement. They said, "Hurray! Today is the big party and we will get presents!"

Sadly, the man said, "No, my dear children. When we were rich, these clothes were only reminders of the time when we were poor. But now we are just as poor as we were then, and I have no other clothes."

The *Dubner Maggid* used this story to explain the difference between the *Seder* of long ago when the *Bais Hamikdash* (Holy Temple in Jerusalem) still stood, and the *Seder* of today.

When we had the *Bais Hamikdash* and were still in *Eretz Yisrael,* the *Korban Pesach* (Passover offering — a lamb or a baby goat) was eaten with matzah at the *Seder.* At that time we were not in *galus* (exile), so the matzos only reminded us of the *galus* long ago in Egypt. In those days we said, "כְּהָא לַחְמָא עַנְיָא, this is *like* the plain, poor bread of *galus.*" But now, when we don't have a *Bais Hamikdash,* we look at the matzah and say, "הָא לַחְמָא עַנְיָא, this is the *same* plain, poor bread" that we ate in Egypt. We are in *galus* now — just as our forefathers were in Egypt.

THE SECOND CUP IS FILLED.

Cover the matzos. In some families, the *Seder* plate is removed from the table.
This is done to make the children curious so that they will ask why this night is different.

The youngest person of the *Seder* asks the Four Questions.

 Why is this night different from all other nights?

מַה נִּשְׁתַּנָּה

הַלַּיְלָה הַזֶּה
מִכָּל הַלֵּילוֹת?

On all other nights
we eat either
chametz or matzah,
but tonight — only matzah!

שֶׁבְּכָל הַלֵּילוֹת
אָנוּ אוֹכְלִין חָמֵץ וּמַצָּה,
הַלַּיְלָה הַזֶּה — כֻּלּוֹ מַצָּה.

On all other nights
we eat any vegetables,
bitter or not bitter,
but tonight —
bitter *marror!*

שֶׁבְּכָל הַלֵּילוֹת
אָנוּ אוֹכְלִין שְׁאָר יְרָקוֹת,
הַלַּיְלָה הַזֶּה — מָרוֹר.

On all other nights
we do not have to
dip our food even once,
but tonight — twice,
once *karpas* in salt-water,
and once *marror* in *charoses!*

שֶׁבְּכָל הַלֵּילוֹת
אֵין אָנוּ מַטְבִּילִין
אֲפִילוּ פַּעַם אֶחָת,
הַלַּיְלָה הַזֶּה — שְׁתֵּי פְעָמִים.

On all other nights
we sit either straight or leaning,
but tonight — we all lean!

שֶׁבְּכָל הַלֵּילוֹת
אָנוּ אוֹכְלִין
בֵּין יוֹשְׁבִין וּבֵין מְסֻבִּין,
הַלַּיְלָה הַזֶּה — כֻּלָּנוּ מְסֻבִּין.

מַה נִּשְׁתַּנָּה הַלַּיְלָה הַזֶּה — **Why is this night different ...?**

All four questions can really be understood as one long question: We eat matzah and *marror,* which remind us that we were slaves; and we dip our food and recline on pillows as if we were kings. How can we be slaves and kings on the same night?

The answer is found in the first sentence after the Four Questions. "We used to be slaves ... but HASHEM ... took us out." In Egypt when our forefathers sat down to the first *Seder* they were still slaves. Then — in the middle of the night — they became free! So we really were like slaves and like kings on the same night. That is part of the miracle that we celebrate at our *Seder.* That is why we act like slaves and like kings at the same time.

הגדה של פסח / 16

We used to be slaves to Pharaoh in Egypt, but HASHEM our God reached out His strong arm and took us out from there. If God had not saved us from Egypt, all of us — even our children and grandchildren — would still be slaves to Pharaoh. So even if we are very smart and know the Torah, it is a *mitzvah* for us to tell about the miracles that happened when the Jews left Egypt. The more someone tells about it, the more he deserves to be praised.

עֲבָדִים הָיִינוּ לְפַרְעֹה בְּמִצְרַיִם, וַיּוֹצִיאֵנוּ יהוה אֱלֹהֵינוּ מִשָּׁם בְּיָד חֲזָקָה וּבִזְרוֹעַ נְטוּיָה. וְאִלּוּ לֹא הוֹצִיא הַקָּדוֹשׁ בָּרוּךְ הוּא אֶת אֲבוֹתֵינוּ מִמִּצְרַיִם, הֲרֵי אָנוּ וּבָנֵינוּ וּבְנֵי בָנֵינוּ מְשֻׁעְבָּדִים הָיִינוּ לְפַרְעֹה בְּמִצְרָיִם. וַאֲפִילוּ כֻּלָּנוּ חֲכָמִים, כֻּלָּנוּ נְבוֹנִים, כֻּלָּנוּ זְקֵנִים, כֻּלָּנוּ יוֹדְעִים אֶת הַתּוֹרָה, מִצְוָה עָלֵינוּ לְסַפֵּר בִּיצִיאַת מִצְרָיִם. וְכָל הַמַּרְבֶּה לְסַפֵּר בִּיצִיאַת מִצְרַיִם, הֲרֵי זֶה מְשֻׁבָּח.

וְכָל הַמַּרְבֶּה לְסַפֵּר — **The more someone tells…**

A ship was caught in a storm and began sinking. All those on board prayed for a miracle — and it happened! Everyone was grateful, but not in the same way. The rich passengers who were in good health and had large families had very much to live for. They were the happiest of all. They told everybody of the great miracle that saved them. Those who were poor, sick, or lonely were also thankful for the miracle. But since their lives remained sad, they didn't speak about the miracle all the time.

It is the same with the miracles of Egypt. If someone can't stop talking about how good God was to us by making us free, it shows that he is very grateful for what God did. Such a person deserves to be praised.

One Seder night, five of the greatest rabbis — Rabbi Eliezer, Rabbi Yehoshua, Rabbi Elazar ben Azaryah, Rabbi Akiva, and Rabbi Tarfon — were sitting in Bnai Brak. All night long they told about the miracles that happened when the Jews left Egypt. They did not stop until their students came to tell them it was time for the morning prayers.

Rabbi Elazar ben Azariah held that it is a *mitzvah* to speak every night (during *Maariv*) about the Jews leaving Egypt. He said, "A miracle happened to make me look as if I were seventy years old, yet I could not prove that we must speak every night about the Jews leaving Egypt. Then Ben Zoma proved it. The Torah states: 'So that you will remember the day you left Egypt **all** the days of your life.' The words 'days of your life' mean the **day**time. The word 'all' means that during all times of the day, even at night, we must speak about leaving Egypt."

But the other rabbis did not agree. They said, "The words 'days of your life' mean that we speak about leaving Egypt now, before *Mashiach* has come. The word 'all' means that we will still speak about leaving Egypt, even after *Mashiach* comes."

מַעֲשֶׂה בְּרַבִּי אֱלִיעֶזֶר וְרַבִּי יְהוֹשֻעַ וְרַבִּי אֶלְעָזָר בֶּן עֲזַרְיָה וְרַבִּי עֲקִיבָא וְרַבִּי טַרְפוֹן שֶׁהָיוּ מְסֻבִּין בִּבְנֵי בְרַק, וְהָיוּ מְסַפְּרִים בִּיצִיאַת מִצְרַיִם כָּל אוֹתוֹ הַלַּיְלָה. עַד שֶׁבָּאוּ תַלְמִידֵיהֶם וְאָמְרוּ לָהֶם, רַבּוֹתֵינוּ הִגִּיעַ זְמַן קְרִיאַת שְׁמַע שֶׁל שַׁחֲרִית.

אָמַר רַבִּי אֶלְעָזָר בֶּן עֲזַרְיָה, הֲרֵי אֲנִי כְּבֶן שִׁבְעִים שָׁנָה, וְלֹא זָכִיתִי שֶׁתֵּאָמֵר יְצִיאַת מִצְרַיִם בַּלֵּילוֹת, עַד שֶׁדְּרָשָׁה בֶּן זוֹמָא, שֶׁנֶּאֱמַר, לְמַעַן תִּזְכֹּר אֶת יוֹם צֵאתְךָ מֵאֶרֶץ מִצְרַיִם כֹּל יְמֵי חַיֶּיךָ. יְמֵי חַיֶּיךָ הַיָּמִים, כֹּל יְמֵי חַיֶּיךָ הַלֵּילוֹת. וַחֲכָמִים אוֹמְרִים, יְמֵי חַיֶּיךָ הָעוֹלָם הַזֶּה, כֹּל יְמֵי חַיֶּיךָ לְהָבִיא לִימוֹת הַמָּשִׁיחַ.

כְּבֶן שִׁבְעִים שָׁנָה — ... As if I were seventy years old ...
Rabbi Elazar ben Azariah was chosen to be the *Nassi* (leader) of the Jewish people when he was only eighteen years old. The Sages feared that the ordinary people who did not know him would not respect such a young man. Then, a great miracle happened. Overnight Rabbi Elazar's face aged, until he looked like an old man of seventy. At that time he said, "A miracle happened to make me look as if I were seventy years old ..."

Blessed is God Who is everywhere — blessed is He!

Blessed is the One Who gave the Torah to His nation, Israel — blessed is He! In the Torah we see that there are four different kinds of children, and we must teach each of them in a different way about Pesach: one is **wise**, one is **evil** one is **simple**, and one doesn't even understand enough to ask questions.

he wise child — what does he say? "I want to know all about the different kinds of *mitzvos* that HASHEM our God told you to do." Since this child wants to learn, you should teach him all the laws of Pesach — up to the last law of the *Seder*: that we are not allowed to eat after the *Afikoman*.

he evil child — what does he say? "Why do **you** go to the trouble of doing these mitzvos?" He thinks that the mitzvos are only for **you**, but not for **him**! Because he doesn't want to be part of us, that proves he doesn't believe in the Torah, so you should give him a very sharp answer. Tell him that the Torah says, "It was because of these *mitzvos* that HASHEM did miracles **for me** when I left Egypt." The Torah says **for me**, but not for people like **him**. If the evil child had been in Egypt, he would not have been saved.

he simple child — what does he say? "What is this all about?" Explain to him, "We do these *mitzvos* because HASHEM used His strong hand to save us from slavery in Egypt."

he child who doesn't even understand enough to ask — you have to start him off. As the Torah says: "You shall tell your child on the day of Pesach, 'It was because of these *mitzvos* that HASHEM did miracles for me when I left Egypt.' "

בָּרוּךְ הַמָּקוֹם, בָּרוּךְ הוּא.

בָּרוּךְ שֶׁנָּתַן תּוֹרָה לְעַמּוֹ יִשְׂרָאֵל, בָּרוּךְ הוּא. כְּנֶגֶד אַרְבָּעָה בָנִים דִּבְּרָה תוֹרָה: אֶחָד חָכָם, וְאֶחָד רָשָׁע, וְאֶחָד תָּם, וְאֶחָד שֶׁאֵינוֹ יוֹדֵעַ לִשְׁאוֹל.

חָכָם מָה הוּא אוֹמֵר? מָה הָעֵדֹת וְהַחֻקִּים וְהַמִּשְׁפָּטִים אֲשֶׁר צִוָּה יהוה אֱלֹהֵינוּ אֶתְכֶם? וְאַף אַתָּה אֱמָר לוֹ כְּהִלְכוֹת הַפֶּסַח, אֵין מַפְטִירִין אַחַר הַפֶּסַח אֲפִיקוֹמָן.

רָשָׁע מָה הוּא אוֹמֵר? מָה הָעֲבֹדָה הַזֹּאת לָכֶם? לָכֶם וְלֹא לוֹ! וּלְפִי שֶׁהוֹצִיא אֶת עַצְמוֹ מִן הַכְּלָל, כָּפַר בְּעִקָּר. וְאַף אַתָּה הַקְהֵה אֶת שִׁנָּיו. וֶאֱמָר לוֹ, בַּעֲבוּר זֶה עָשָׂה יהוה לִי בְּצֵאתִי מִמִּצְרָיִם, לִי וְלֹא לוֹ, אִלּוּ הָיָה שָׁם לֹא הָיָה נִגְאָל.

תָּם מָה הוּא אוֹמֵר? מָה זֹּאת? וְאָמַרְתָּ אֵלָיו, בְּחֹזֶק יָד הוֹצִיאָנוּ יהוה מִמִּצְרַיִם מִבֵּית עֲבָדִים.

וְשֶׁאֵינוֹ יוֹדֵעַ לִשְׁאוֹל, אַתְּ פְּתַח לוֹ. שֶׁנֶּאֱמַר, וְהִגַּדְתָּ לְבִנְךָ בַּיּוֹם הַהוּא לֵאמֹר, בַּעֲבוּר זֶה עָשָׂה יהוה לִי בְּצֵאתִי מִמִּצְרָיִם.

אַרְבָּעָה בָנִים — Four different kinds of children.
The Torah and the Haggadah stress that the story of the miracles be told to our children. One reason for this is that our children gained more than anyone else when God saved us from Egypt. Pharaoh once ordered the midwives to kill each new-born boy. Then he commanded the people to drown the baby boys. Another time he tried to stop the Jews from having children. If the Jews couldn't make enough bricks, the Egyptians put Jewish children into the walls. There was a time when Pharaoh used to kill Jewish babies to bathe in their blood. The troubles for the Jewish children finally ended when God took us out of Egypt. That is why the story of the miracles of leaving Egypt is directed most of all to our children.

Perhaps we should start telling about the miracles of leaving Egypt on the first day of Nissan (because that was when Moses taught the *mitzvah* of Pesach)? But the Torah says "You shall tell your child **on that day**," meaning the day of the Pesach offering. [The Pesach offering was brought on the afternoon before the Pesach holiday.] If so, perhaps we should tell of the miracles on the afternoon before the *Seder*? But the Torah continues that we should say, "**It is because of this**," meaning because of something you can point to. That cannot be said until the *Seder* when the matzah and *marror* are on the table in front of you.

In very ancient times, our ancestors used to serve idols, but now HASHEM drew us near to serve Him. As the Prophet says, "Joshua told the Jewish people that HASHEM, God of Israel, said, 'Terach, father of Abraham and Nachor, lived across the river and he used to serve idols. But I took Abraham away from across the river and brought him to *Eretz Yisrael*. I gave him many children and grandchildren. First I gave him Isaac. To Isaac, I gave two sons, Jacob and Esau, but to Esau I gave Mount Seir (south of *Eretz Yisrael*) for his homeland, while Jacob and his children had to go down to Egypt.'"

יָכוֹל מֵרֹאשׁ חֹדֶשׁ, תַּלְמוּד לוֹמַר בַּיּוֹם הַהוּא. אִי בַּיּוֹם הַהוּא, יָכוֹל מִבְּעוֹד יוֹם, תַּלְמוּד לוֹמַר בַּעֲבוּר זֶה. בַּעֲבוּר זֶה לֹא אָמַרְתִּי אֶלָּא בְּשָׁעָה שֶׁיֵּשׁ מַצָּה וּמָרוֹר מֻנָּחִים לְפָנֶיךָ.

מִתְּחִלָּה, עוֹבְדֵי עֲבוֹדָה זָרָה הָיוּ אֲבוֹתֵינוּ, וְעַכְשָׁו קֵרְבָנוּ הַמָּקוֹם לַעֲבוֹדָתוֹ. שֶׁנֶּאֱמַר, וַיֹּאמֶר יְהוֹשֻׁעַ אֶל כָּל הָעָם, כֹּה אָמַר יהוה אֱלֹהֵי יִשְׂרָאֵל, בְּעֵבֶר הַנָּהָר יָשְׁבוּ אֲבוֹתֵיכֶם מֵעוֹלָם, תֶּרַח אֲבִי אַבְרָהָם וַאֲבִי נָחוֹר, וַיַּעַבְדוּ אֱלֹהִים אֲחֵרִים. וָאֶקַּח אֶת אֲבִיכֶם אֶת אַבְרָהָם מֵעֵבֶר הַנָּהָר, וָאוֹלֵךְ אוֹתוֹ בְּכָל אֶרֶץ כְּנָעַן, וָאַרְבֶּה אֶת זַרְעוֹ, וָאֶתֶּן לוֹ אֶת יִצְחָק. וָאֶתֵּן לְיִצְחָק אֶת יַעֲקֹב וְאֶת עֵשָׂו, וָאֶתֵּן לְעֵשָׂו אֶת הַר שֵׂעִיר לָרֶשֶׁת אוֹתוֹ, וְיַעֲקֹב וּבָנָיו יָרְדוּ מִצְרָיִם.

Blessed is God Who keeps His promise to Israel, blessed is He! God calculated the right time to save us from Egypt and keep His promise to Abraham. As He had told Abraham at the Covenant Between the Parts: "You should know that your children will be strangers in a foreign land. The people of the land will force them to be slaves and will make them suffer; all this will take four hundred years. But I

בָּרוּךְ שׁוֹמֵר הַבְטָחָתוֹ לְיִשְׂרָאֵל, בָּרוּךְ הוּא. שֶׁהַקָּדוֹשׁ בָּרוּךְ הוּא חִשַּׁב אֶת הַקֵּץ, לַעֲשׂוֹת כְּמָה שֶׁאָמַר לְאַבְרָהָם אָבִינוּ בִּבְרִית בֵּין הַבְּתָרִים, שֶׁנֶּאֱמַר, וַיֹּאמֶר לְאַבְרָם, יָדֹעַ תֵּדַע כִּי גֵר יִהְיֶה זַרְעֲךָ בְּאֶרֶץ לֹא לָהֶם, וַעֲבָדוּם וְעִנּוּ אֹתָם, אַרְבַּע מֵאוֹת

will punish the nation that will make them slaves — and then your children will go free with a great fortune."

שָׁנָה. וְגַם אֶת הַגּוֹי אֲשֶׁר יַעֲבֹדוּ דָּן אָנֹכִי, וְאַחֲרֵי כֵן יֵצְאוּ בִּרְכֻשׁ גָּדוֹל.

Cover the matzos. Everyone should raise his cup and recite the next paragraph with great joy.

It is that promise to Abraham that protected

וְהִיא שֶׁעָמְדָה

our fathers and us, because more than one nation has tried to destroy us. In every generation they try to destroy us, but God always saves us from them.

לַאֲבוֹתֵינוּ וְלָנוּ, שֶׁלֹּא אֶחָד בִּלְבָד עָמַד עָלֵינוּ לְכַלּוֹתֵנוּ. אֶלָּא שֶׁבְּכָל דּוֹר וָדוֹר עוֹמְדִים עָלֵינוּ לְכַלּוֹתֵנוּ, וְהַקָּדוֹשׁ בָּרוּךְ הוּא מַצִּילֵנוּ מִיָּדָם.

Put down the cup and uncover the matzos.

Let us look at the Torah and see the kind of dangers that God saved us from. Jacob had to deal with Laban who was even more dangerous than Pharaoh. Pharaoh ordered that only the boy babies should be killed, but Laban had tried to destroy Jacob's whole family, as the Torah says:

Laban the Aramean tried to destroy my father, Jacob. After that Jacob went down to Egypt and stayed for a while, with just a few people, and there he became a nation — great, strong, and big.

צֵא וּלְמַד מַה בִּקֵּשׁ לָבָן הָאֲרַמִּי לַעֲשׂוֹת לְיַעֲקֹב אָבִינוּ, שֶׁפַּרְעֹה לֹא גָזַר אֶלָּא עַל הַזְּכָרִים, וְלָבָן בִּקֵּשׁ לַעֲקוֹר אֶת הַכֹּל. שֶׁנֶּאֱמַר:

אֲרַמִּי אֹבֵד אָבִי, וַיֵּרֶד מִצְרַיְמָה וַיָּגָר שָׁם בִּמְתֵי מְעָט, וַיְהִי שָׁם לְגוֹי, גָּדוֹל עָצוּם וָרָב.

וְהִיא שֶׁעָמְדָה — **It protected …**

God's promise saved us from being completely destroyed by our enemies, through all the years — from Pharaoh to Haman to Hitler.

God made this promise because He knew that we would remain true to Him, we would study His Torah, and we would keep His *mitzvos*. This is hinted to in the letters of the word וְהִיא.

ו=6. The Six Sections of the Mishnah.

ה=5. The five *Chumashim*.

י=10. The Ten Commandments.

א=1. HASHEM, the One and Only God.

לָבָן בִּקֵּשׁ לַעֲקוֹר אֶת הַכֹּל — **Laban had tried to destroy Jacob's whole family.**

Laban said that all Jacob's wives and children really belonged to Laban. If he had been able to get his way, he would have trained all the Jews to serve his idols and be like him. Had he succeeded, there would never have been a Jewish people.

[Now the *Haggadah* explains each part of that verse in which the Torah tells us about Jacob going to Egypt.]

After that Jacob went down to Egypt — he was forced to go by God's command.

And stayed for a while — this teaches us that our father Jacob did not go down to Egypt to settle there, but only to stay for a short while. As the Torah says: "Jacob's sons told Pharaoh, 'We have come to live here for a while, because there is no grass for our sheep in the land of Canaan, since the hunger is very bad in Canaan. So now, please let us, your servants, live in the land of Goshen.'"

With just a few people — as the Torah says: "With seventy people your ancestors went down to Egypt, and now HASHEM your God has made you as many as the stars of heaven."

And there he became a nation — this teaches that the Jews did not become just like the Egyptians. You could look at people and tell which ones were Jewish.

Great, strong — as the Torah says: "And the Jewish people had many children and increased very much and multiplied. They became very, very strong and the country was filled with them."

And big — the Torah speaks about the Jewish people as if they were a little girl who grew up. God said: "I made you grow big like the plants of the field, and you grew big and tall. You became beautiful with long hair — but since you had no *mitzvos*, it was as if you had no clothes to wear. [Then God gave us two *mitzvos*, both of which involved blood — the blood of *bris milah* and the blood of the Pesach offering; and then He said:] I said to you, 'You will live because of your blood! You will live because of your blood!'"

וַיֵּרֶד מִצְרַיְמָה — אָנוּס עַל פִּי הַדִּבּוּר.

וַיָּגָר שָׁם — מְלַמֵּד שֶׁלֹּא יָרַד יַעֲקֹב אָבִינוּ לְהִשְׁתַּקֵּעַ בְּמִצְרַיִם, אֶלָּא לָגוּר שָׁם. שֶׁנֶּאֱמַר, וַיֹּאמְרוּ אֶל פַּרְעֹה, לָגוּר בָּאָרֶץ בָּאנוּ, כִּי אֵין מִרְעֶה לַצֹּאן אֲשֶׁר לַעֲבָדֶיךָ, כִּי כָבֵד הָרָעָב בְּאֶרֶץ כְּנָעַן, וְעַתָּה יֵשְׁבוּ נָא עֲבָדֶיךָ בְּאֶרֶץ גֹּשֶׁן.

בִּמְתֵי מְעָט — כְּמָה שֶׁנֶּאֱמַר, בְּשִׁבְעִים נֶפֶשׁ יָרְדוּ אֲבֹתֶיךָ מִצְרַיְמָה, וְעַתָּה שָׂמְךָ יהוה אֱלֹהֶיךָ כְּכוֹכְבֵי הַשָּׁמַיִם לָרֹב.

וַיְהִי שָׁם לְגוֹי — מְלַמֵּד שֶׁהָיוּ יִשְׂרָאֵל מְצֻיָּנִים שָׁם.

גָּדוֹל עָצוּם — כְּמָה שֶׁנֶּאֱמַר, וּבְנֵי יִשְׂרָאֵל פָּרוּ וַיִּשְׁרְצוּ וַיִּרְבּוּ וַיַּעַצְמוּ בִּמְאֹד מְאֹד, וַתִּמָּלֵא הָאָרֶץ אֹתָם.

וָרָב — כְּמָה שֶׁנֶּאֱמַר, רְבָבָה כְּצֶמַח הַשָּׂדֶה נְתַתִּיךְ, וַתִּרְבִּי וַתִּגְדְּלִי וַתָּבֹאִי בַּעֲדִי עֲדָיִים, שָׁדַיִם נָכֹנוּ וּשְׂעָרֵךְ צִמֵּחַ, וְאַתְּ עֵרֹם וְעֶרְיָה; וָאֶעֱבֹר עָלַיִךְ וָאֶרְאֵךְ מִתְבּוֹסֶסֶת בְּדָמָיִךְ, וָאֹמַר לָךְ, בְּדָמַיִךְ חֲיִי, וָאֹמַר לָךְ, בְּדָמַיִךְ חֲיִי.

[The Torah continues with the story of our ancestors' slavery in Egypt:]

The Egyptians were bad to us, they made us suffer and made us do hard work.

[Now the *Haggadah* explains each part of the verse:]

The Egyptians were bad to us —as the Torah says: "The Egyptians said, 'Come, let us outsmart the Jews, otherwise there will be so many

וַיָּרֵעוּ אֹתָנוּ הַמִּצְרִים, וַיְעַנּוּנוּ, וַיִּתְּנוּ עָלֵינוּ עֲבֹדָה קָשָׁה.

וַיָּרֵעוּ אֹתָנוּ הַמִּצְרִים— כְּמָה שֶׁנֶּאֱמַר, הָבָה נִתְחַכְּמָה לוֹ, פֶּן יִרְבֶּה, וְהָיָה כִּי

of them that in case of war, they will join our enemies, and they will fight us and leave our country.' "

They made us suffer — as the Torah says: "The Egyptians set up masters over the Jews to make them suffer with hard work, and the Jews built treasure-cities for Pharaoh. The cities were called Pisom and Raameses."

And they made us do hard work — as the Torah says: "The Egyptians forced the Jews to do backbreaking work."

[The Torah continues the story of our ancestors' slavery:]

**We cried out to HASHEM,
the God of our ancestors.
HASHEM heard our cry,
and He saw our suffering,
our misery,
and our oppression.**

[Now the Haggadah explains each part of the verse:]

We cried out to HASHEM the God of our ancestors — as the Torah says: "It happened during that long time that the King of Egypt died. The Jewish people groaned from the work and they cried out. Their cries from the work went up to God."

HASHEM heard our cry — as the Torah says: "And God heard their moaning; and God remembered His agreement with Abraham, Isaac and Jacob."

And He saw our suffering — this means that the Egyptians broke up Jewish family life, as the Torah says: "God saw what was happening to the Jewish people and God knew what He had to do."

And our misery — This is the misery of what the Egyptians did to our sons, as the Torah says: "Pharaoh commanded, 'Throw every newborn boy into the river, and let every girl live!'"

And our oppression — this means that they never let us relax, as the Torah says: "God said, 'I have seen how the Egyptians oppress them, not letting them relax.' "

תִּקְרֶאנָה מִלְחָמָה, וְנוֹסַף גַּם הוּא עַל שֹׂנְאֵינוּ, וְנִלְחַם בָּנוּ, וְעָלָה מִן הָאָרֶץ.

וַיְעַנּוּנוּ — כְּמָה שֶׁנֶּאֱמַר, וַיָּשִׂימוּ עָלָיו שָׂרֵי מִסִּים, לְמַעַן עַנֹּתוֹ בְּסִבְלֹתָם, וַיִּבֶן עָרֵי מִסְכְּנוֹת לְפַרְעֹה, אֶת פִּתֹם וְאֶת רַעַמְסֵס.

וַיִּתְּנוּ עָלֵינוּ עֲבֹדָה קָשָׁה — כְּמָה שֶׁנֶּאֱמַר, וַיַּעֲבִדוּ מִצְרַיִם אֶת בְּנֵי יִשְׂרָאֵל בְּפָרֶךְ.

וַנִּצְעַק אֶל יהוה אֱלֹהֵי אֲבֹתֵינוּ, וַיִּשְׁמַע יהוה אֶת קֹלֵנוּ, וַיַּרְא אֶת עָנְיֵנוּ, וְאֶת עֲמָלֵנוּ, וְאֶת לַחֲצֵנוּ.

וַנִּצְעַק אֶל יהוה אֱלֹהֵי אֲבֹתֵינוּ — כְּמָה שֶׁנֶּאֱמַר, וַיְהִי בַיָּמִים הָרַבִּים הָהֵם, וַיָּמָת מֶלֶךְ מִצְרַיִם, וַיֵּאָנְחוּ בְנֵי יִשְׂרָאֵל מִן הָעֲבֹדָה, וַיִּזְעָקוּ, וַתַּעַל שַׁוְעָתָם אֶל הָאֱלֹהִים מִן הָעֲבֹדָה.

וַיִּשְׁמַע יהוה אֶת קֹלֵנוּ — כְּמָה שֶׁנֶּאֱמַר, וַיִּשְׁמַע אֱלֹהִים אֶת נַאֲקָתָם, וַיִּזְכֹּר אֱלֹהִים אֶת בְּרִיתוֹ אֶת אַבְרָהָם, אֶת יִצְחָק, וְאֶת יַעֲקֹב.

וַיַּרְא אֶת עָנְיֵנוּ — זוֹ פְּרִישׁוּת דֶּרֶךְ אֶרֶץ, כְּמָה שֶׁנֶּאֱמַר, וַיַּרְא אֱלֹהִים אֶת בְּנֵי יִשְׂרָאֵל, וַיֵּדַע אֱלֹהִים.

וְאֶת עֲמָלֵנוּ — אֵלּוּ הַבָּנִים, כְּמָה שֶׁנֶּאֱמַר, כָּל הַבֵּן הַיִּלּוֹד הַיְאֹרָה תַּשְׁלִיכֻהוּ, וְכָל הַבַּת תְּחַיּוּן.

וְאֶת לַחֲצֵנוּ — זוֹ הַדְּחַק, כְּמָה שֶׁנֶּאֱמַר, וְגַם רָאִיתִי אֶת הַלַּחַץ אֲשֶׁר מִצְרַיִם לֹחֲצִים אֹתָם.

[The Torah continues the story of our ancestors' slavery:]

And HASHEM took us out of Egypt with a strong hand, with an outstretched arm, with great fear, with signs and with miracles.

וַיּוֹצִאֵנוּ יהוה מִמִּצְרַיִם בְּיָד חֲזָקָה, וּבִזְרֹעַ נְטוּיָה, וּבְמֹרָא גָּדֹל, וּבְאֹתוֹת וּבְמֹפְתִים.

[Now the *Haggadah* explains each part of the verse:]

And HASHEM took us out of Egypt — He didn't do it through any kind of angel or messenger; God **Himself** took us out, as the Torah says: "God said, 'I will go through the land of Egypt on this night of Pesach and I will strike every firstborn in Egypt — people and animals — and I will break all the Egyptian idols; I am HASHEM.' "

When God said: "I will go through the land of Egypt," it is as if He said, "I will go Myself — I will not send an angel."

When He said, "I will strike every firstborn in Egypt," it is as if He said, "I will do it Myself — I will not send a flaming angel."

When He said, "And I will break all the Egyptian idols," it is as if He said, "I will do it Myself — I will not send a messenger."

When He said, "I am HASHEM," it is as if He said, "I will do it Myself — and no one else!"

וַיּוֹצִאֵנוּ יהוה מִמִּצְרַיִם — לֹא עַל יְדֵי מַלְאָךְ, וְלֹא עַל יְדֵי שָׂרָף, וְלֹא עַל יְדֵי שָׁלִיחַ, אֶלָּא הַקָּדוֹשׁ בָּרוּךְ הוּא בִּכְבוֹדוֹ וּבְעַצְמוֹ. שֶׁנֶּאֱמַר, וְעָבַרְתִּי בְאֶרֶץ מִצְרַיִם בַּלַּיְלָה הַזֶּה, וְהִכֵּיתִי כָל בְּכוֹר בְּאֶרֶץ מִצְרַיִם מֵאָדָם וְעַד בְּהֵמָה, וּבְכָל אֱלֹהֵי מִצְרַיִם אֶעֱשֶׂה שְׁפָטִים, אֲנִי יהוה.

וְעָבַרְתִּי בְאֶרֶץ מִצְרַיִם בַּלַּיְלָה הַזֶּה — אֲנִי וְלֹא מַלְאָךְ.

וְהִכֵּיתִי כָל בְּכוֹר בְּאֶרֶץ מִצְרַיִם — אֲנִי וְלֹא שָׂרָף.

וּבְכָל אֱלֹהֵי מִצְרַיִם אֶעֱשֶׂה שְׁפָטִים — אֲנִי וְלֹא הַשָּׁלִיחַ.

אֲנִי יהוה — אֲנִי הוּא, וְלֹא אַחֵר.

וּבְמוֹרָא גָּדֹל — And with great fear.
Why are people frightened when God shows His Presence? People are not afraid if they are in control of a situation. But when God shows us His greatness, we realize that He has the power to do whatever He wants, whether we like it or not.

וּבְאֹתוֹת — And with signs.
God makes "signs" to prove that He does as He wishes. In Egypt, the signs were that Moses told Pharaoh in advance what every plague would be. No human being could ever have predicted such things.
Another meaning of אֹתוֹת is "letters." The *Midrash* teaches that the initials of the Ten Plagues were carved into Moses' stick. This is what R' Yehudah means (see the next page) when he arranges the plagues into sets: דְּצַ"ךְ עַדַ"שׁ בְּאַחַ"ב.

This is how the letters were written on the stick. Anyone who looked at those letters and then saw how the plagues actually happened had to say, "This is a sign that God decides beforehand what will take place. Even though Aaron made the first plagues come about, and Moses did not use the stick for each plague, the plagues happened in the exact order that they appeared on that miraculous stick that God gave to Moses."

וּבְמֹפְתִים — And with miracles.
The word "miracles" means anything that changes the laws of nature. In Egypt, the miracles were the plagues themselves. When the *Haggadah* states that וּבְמֹפְתִים stands for blood, it means that God changed the laws of nature by turning all the water into blood.

With a strong hand — this stands for the plague that killed animals, as the Torah says: "HASHEM's **hand** will be on your cattle in the field, on the horses, the donkeys, the camels, the cattle, and the sheep — a very harsh plague."

With an outstretched arm this stands for "the sword," which is another way of saying that people will be killed. In telling of a plague that killed 70,000 people in Jerusalem, the Torah says: "[King David saw an angel] with a drawn sword in his hand, **outstretched** over Jerusalem."

And with great awe — this stands for the awe that people feel when they are in God's Presence, as the Torah says: "Did God ever come and take one nation out from the middle of another nation — using signs and miracles, a strong hand and an outstretched arm, with great and awe-inspiring deeds — as HASHEM your God did for you before your very eyes in Egypt?"

And with signs — this stands for the stick that Moses used to make miracles, as the Torah says: God told Moses, "Take this stick in your hand, and use it to make the signs."

And with wonders — this stands for the plague of blood, as the Torah says: God said, "I will make wonders in heaven and on earth — and these wonders will be:

As each of the words דָּם, *blood*, אֵשׁ, *fire*, and עָשָׁן, *smoke*, is said, remove a bit of wine from the cup, with the finger or by pouring.

Blood and fire and pillars of smoke."

[The wonder on earth will be blood, and the wonder in heaven will be fire and smoke.]

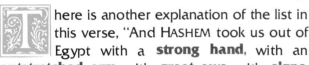 here is another explanation of the list in this verse, "And HASHEM took us out of Egypt with a **strong hand**, with an **outstretched arm**, with **great awe**, with **signs**, and with **wonders**." Each of the five phrases listed in the verse either contains two words or is in plural, which also stands for two. This adds up to ten — the Ten Plagues that God brought upon the Egyptians in Egypt. The Ten Plagues are:

בְּיָד חֲזָקָה — זוֹ הַדֶּבֶר, כְּמָה שֶׁנֶּאֱמַר, הִנֵּה יַד יהוה הוֹיָה בְּמִקְנְךָ אֲשֶׁר בַּשָּׂדֶה, בַּסּוּסִים בַּחֲמֹרִים בַּגְּמַלִּים בַּבָּקָר וּבַצֹּאן, דֶּבֶר כָּבֵד מְאֹד.

וּבִזְרֹעַ נְטוּיָה — זוֹ הַחֶרֶב, כְּמָה שֶׁנֶּאֱמַר, וְחַרְבּוֹ שְׁלוּפָה בְּיָדוֹ, נְטוּיָה עַל יְרוּשָׁלָיִם.

וּבְמֹרָא גָּדֹל — זוֹ גִּלּוּי שְׁכִינָה, כְּמָה שֶׁנֶּאֱמַר, אוֹ הֲנִסָּה אֱלֹהִים לָבוֹא לָקַחַת לוֹ גוֹי מִקֶּרֶב גּוֹי, בְּמַסֹּת, בְּאֹתֹת, וּבְמוֹפְתִים, וּבְמִלְחָמָה, וּבְיָד חֲזָקָה, וּבִזְרֹעַ נְטוּיָה, וּבְמוֹרָאִים גְּדֹלִים, כְּכֹל אֲשֶׁר עָשָׂה לָכֶם יהוה אֱלֹהֵיכֶם בְּמִצְרַיִם לְעֵינֶיךָ.

וּבְאֹתוֹת — זֶה הַמַּטֶּה, כְּמָה שֶׁנֶּאֱמַר, וְאֶת הַמַּטֶּה הַזֶּה תִּקַּח בְּיָדֶךָ, אֲשֶׁר תַּעֲשֶׂה בּוֹ אֶת הָאֹתֹת.

וּבְמֹפְתִים — זֶה הַדָּם, כְּמָה שֶׁנֶּאֱמַר, וְנָתַתִּי מוֹפְתִים בַּשָּׁמַיִם וּבָאָרֶץ

דָם • וָאֵשׁ • וְתִמְרוֹת עָשָׁן.

דָּבָר אַחֵר — בְּיָד חֲזָקָה, שְׁתַּיִם. וּבִזְרֹעַ נְטוּיָה, שְׁתַּיִם. וּבְמֹרָא גָּדֹל, שְׁתַּיִם. וּבְאֹתוֹת, שְׁתַּיִם. וּבְמֹפְתִים, שְׁתַּיִם. אֵלּוּ עֶשֶׂר מַכּוֹת שֶׁהֵבִיא הַקָּדוֹשׁ בָּרוּךְ הוּא עַל הַמִּצְרִים בְּמִצְרַיִם, וְאֵלּוּ הֵן:

עֶשֶׂר מַכּוֹת — The Ten Plagues.

Why do we remove a drop of wine from our cups when we mention each of the Ten Plagues?

The *Midrash* tells us that when God split the Sea of Reeds to save us and then to drown the Egyptians, the angels in heaven wanted to sing praises — but God didn't let them. He said to them , "My creatures are drowning in the sea and you wish to sing?" From this we learn that it is wrong to rejoice when other people die — even bad people! King Solomon taught us: "When your enemy falls, do not be glad; when he trips, do not rejoice."

That is why we take some wine out of our cups when we say the names of the plagues. We don't want our cups to be full when we tell about other people's pain.

As each of the Plagues is mentioned, remove a bit of wine from the cup.
The same is done at each word of Rabbi Yehudah's abbreviation.

BLOOD • FROGS • LICE • WILD ANIMALS

DEATH OF CATTLE • BOILS • HAIL • LOCUSTS

DARKNESS • DEATH OF THE FIRSTBORN.

Rabbi Yehudah arranged the plagues into sets, according to the initials of their Hebrew names:

DETZACH • ADASH • BE'ACHAB.

דָּם • צְפַרְדֵּעַ • כִּנִּים • עָרוֹב
דֶּבֶר • שְׁחִין • בָּרָד • אַרְבֶּה
חֹשֶׁךְ • מַכַּת בְּכוֹרוֹת.

רַבִּי יְהוּדָה הָיָה נוֹתֵן בָּהֶם סִמָּנִים:

דְּצַ"ךְ • עֲדַ"שׁ • בְּאַחַ"ב.

Refill the wine cups, but do not pour back the wine that was removed.

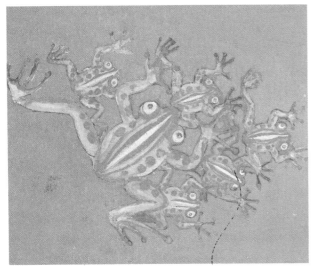

FROGS — צְפַרְדֵּעַ

BLOOD — דָּם

WILD ANIMALS — עָרוֹב

LICE — כִּנִּים

BOILS — שְׁחִין

DEATH OF CATTLE — דֶּבֶר

LOCUSTS — אַרְבֶּה

HAIL — בָּרָד

DEATH OF THE FIRSTBORN — מַכַּת בְּכוֹרוֹת

DARKNESS — חֹשֶׁךְ

Rabbi Yose HaGelili says: How do you know that God punished the Egyptians five times as much at the Sea of Reeds as He did in Egypt — and since there were **ten** plagues in Egypt, there must have been fifty at the Sea? When the Torah speaks about Egypt, it says: "The magicians told Pharaoh, 'This plague is like God's **finger**.'" But when it speaks about the Sea, the Torah says: "The Jewish people saw the great **hand** that HASHEM laid upon Egypt, and they believed in HASHEM and in His servant Moses." How many plagues did the Egyptians suffer in Egypt with HASHEM's **finger**? — Ten. If so, at the Sea (where they were struck with a full **hand** of five fingers) they were struck with fifty plagues (10×5=50).

Rabbi Eliezer says: How do we know that every plague that God brought on the Egyptians in Egypt had four different parts? Because when the Torah speaks about the plagues, it says: "God sent against the Egyptians His burning anger [this means that each plague is a kind of 'burning anger'; now the verse goes on, saying that this 'burning anger' had four parts]: (1) rage, (2) annoyance, (3) trouble, and (4) a troop of bad angels. Since each of the Ten Plagues in Egypt had four parts, it was as if the Ten Plagues were forty plagues (10 plagues×4 parts=40 plagues). And the fifty plagues at the Sea were like two hundred plagues (50 plagues×4 parts =200 plagues).

רַבִּי יוֹסֵי הַגְּלִילִי אוֹמֵר: מִנַּיִן אַתָּה אוֹמֵר שֶׁלָּקוּ הַמִּצְרִים בְּמִצְרַיִם עֶשֶׂר מַכּוֹת וְעַל הַיָּם לָקוּ חֲמִשִּׁים מַכּוֹת? בְּמִצְרַיִם מָה הוּא אוֹמֵר, וַיֹּאמְרוּ הַחַרְטֻמִּם אֶל פַּרְעֹה, אֶצְבַּע אֱלֹהִים הוּא. וְעַל הַיָּם מָה הוּא אוֹמֵר, וַיַּרְא יִשְׂרָאֵל אֶת הַיָּד הַגְּדֹלָה אֲשֶׁר עָשָׂה יהוה בְּמִצְרַיִם, וַיִּירְאוּ הָעָם אֶת יהוה, וַיַּאֲמִינוּ בַּיהוה וּבְמֹשֶׁה עַבְדּוֹ. כַּמָּה לָקוּ בְאֶצְבַּע? עֶשֶׂר מַכּוֹת. אֱמוֹר מֵעַתָּה, בְּמִצְרַיִם לָקוּ עֶשֶׂר מַכּוֹת, וְעַל הַיָּם לָקוּ חֲמִשִּׁים מַכּוֹת.

רַבִּי אֱלִיעֶזֶר אוֹמֵר. מִנַּיִן שֶׁכָּל מַכָּה וּמַכָּה שֶׁהֵבִיא הַקָּדוֹשׁ בָּרוּךְ הוּא עַל הַמִּצְרִים בְּמִצְרַיִם הָיְתָה שֶׁל אַרְבַּע מַכּוֹת? שֶׁנֶּאֱמַר, יְשַׁלַּח בָּם חֲרוֹן אַפּוֹ — עֶבְרָה, וָזַעַם, וְצָרָה, מִשְׁלַחַת מַלְאֲכֵי רָעִים. עֶבְרָה, אַחַת. וָזַעַם, שְׁתַּיִם. וְצָרָה, שָׁלֹשׁ. מִשְׁלַחַת מַלְאֲכֵי רָעִים, אַרְבַּע. אֱמוֹר מֵעַתָּה, בְּמִצְרַיִם לָקוּ אַרְבָּעִים מַכּוֹת, וְעַל הַיָּם לָקוּ מָאתַיִם מַכּוֹת.

עֶשֶׂר מַכּוֹת ... חֲמִשִּׁים מַכּוֹת — Ten plagues ... fifty plagues.

After God took us out of Egypt, He promised that if we would obey the Torah, then "כָּל הַמַּחֲלָה אֲשֶׁר שַׂמְתִּי בְמִצְרַיִם לֹא אָשִׂים עָלֶיךָ, the entire illness that I placed upon Egypt I will not place upon you."

In order to be thankful for a blessing, we have to know how great the blessing is. For example, if someone stops a dog from barking the whole night, he saves us from getting an ordinary headache. We will thank him, but we will not be *very* grateful, because a headache is not a terrible illness. But if someone stops a pack of wild dogs from attacking us, he saves us from injuries that could keep us screaming with pain and in a hospital for many months. We would be so grateful that we could never thank the person enough.

God promised to save us from the kind of suffering the Egyptians had suffered. In order to thank Him properly, it is important for us to know how much the Egyptians suffered. Therefore each of the Rabbis shows that the Egyptian plagues was much worse than it seems.

First, Rabbi Yose tells us that there were not just ten plagues. There were really ten in Egypt and fifty more at the Sea. So there were sixty plagues altogether. Rabbi Eliezer adds that each plague had four parts. So there were 240 plagues in all. Rabbi Akiva shows that each plague had five parts. This means that God promised to save us from 300 plagues.

Since we know how many plagues there really were, we realize how important it is for us to be very thankful to God. And we show our thanks by praising Him and by keeping the Torah and *mitzvos* very carefully.

[Rabbi Eliezer has just said that each plague was called "burning anger," and it had four separate parts. But Rabbi Akiva says that each plague had five different parts, and "burning anger" was only one of the five.]

Rabbi Akiva says: How do we know that every plague that God brought on the Egyptians in Egypt had five different parts? Because the Torah describes the plagues by saying, "God sent against the Egyptians (1) His burning anger, (2) rage, (3) annoyance, (4) trouble, and (5) a troop of bad angels." Since each of the Ten Plagues in Egypt had five parts, it was as if the ten plagues were fifty plagues (10 plagues×5 parts=50 plagues). And the fifty plagues at the Sea were like two hundred fifty plagues (50 plagues×5 parts =250 plagues).

רַבִּי עֲקִיבָא אוֹמֵר. מִנַּיִן שֶׁכָּל מַכָּה וּמַכָּה שֶׁהֵבִיא הַקָּדוֹשׁ בָּרוּךְ הוּא עַל הַמִּצְרִים בְּמִצְרַיִם הָיְתָה שֶׁל חָמֵשׁ מַכּוֹת? שֶׁנֶּאֱמַר, יְשַׁלַּח בָּם חֲרוֹן אַפּוֹ, עֶבְרָה, וָזַעַם, וְצָרָה, מִשְׁלַחַת מַלְאֲכֵי רָעִים. חֲרוֹן אַפּוֹ, אַחַת. עֶבְרָה, שְׁתַּיִם. וָזַעַם, שָׁלֹשׁ. וְצָרָה, אַרְבַּע. מִשְׁלַחַת מַלְאֲכֵי רָעִים, חָמֵשׁ. אֱמוֹר מֵעַתָּה, בְּמִצְרַיִם לָקוּ חֲמִשִּׁים מַכּוֹת, וְעַל הַיָּם לָקוּ חֲמִשִּׁים וּמָאתַיִם מַכּוֹת.

[Now that we have finished our short summary of what happened in Egypt, we begin to praise God.]

God has done so many favors for us!

כַּמָּה מַעֲלוֹת טוֹבוֹת לַמָּקוֹם עָלֵינוּ.

If He had just taken us out of Egypt,
  but not punished the Egyptians,
    it would have been enough for us!

אִלּוּ הוֹצִיאָנוּ מִמִּצְרַיִם,
וְלֹא עָשָׂה בָהֶם שְׁפָטִים, דַּיֵּנוּ.

If He had just punished them,
  but not destroyed their idols,
    it would have been enough for us!

אִלּוּ עָשָׂה בָהֶם שְׁפָטִים,
וְלֹא עָשָׂה בֵאלֹהֵיהֶם, דַּיֵּנוּ.

If He had just destroyed their idols,
  but not killed their firstborn,
    it would have been enough for us!

אִלּוּ עָשָׂה בֵאלֹהֵיהֶם,
וְלֹא הָרַג אֶת בְּכוֹרֵיהֶם, דַּיֵּנוּ.

If He had just killed their firstborn,
  but not given us their wealth,
    it would have been enough for us!

אִלּוּ הָרַג אֶת בְּכוֹרֵיהֶם,
וְלֹא נָתַן לָנוּ אֶת מָמוֹנָם, דַּיֵּנוּ.

If He had just given us their wealth,
  but not split the Sea for us,
    it would have been enough for us!

אִלּוּ נָתַן לָנוּ אֶת מָמוֹנָם,
וְלֹא קָרַע לָנוּ אֶת הַיָּם, דַּיֵּנוּ.

If He had just split the Sea for us,
  but not brought us across it on dry land,
    it would have been enough for us!

אִלּוּ קָרַע לָנוּ אֶת הַיָּם,
וְלֹא הֶעֱבִירָנוּ בְתוֹכוֹ בֶּחָרָבָה, דַּיֵּנוּ.

If He had just brought us across it on dry land,
  but not drowned our enemies in it,
    it would have been enough for us!

אִלּוּ הֶעֱבִירָנוּ בְתוֹכוֹ בֶּחָרָבָה,
וְלֹא שִׁקַּע צָרֵינוּ בְּתוֹכוֹ, דַּיֵּנוּ.

If He had just drowned our enemies in it,
  but not given us everything we needed
  in the desert for forty years,
    it would have been enough for us!

אִלּוּ שִׁקַּע צָרֵינוּ בְּתוֹכוֹ,
וְלֹא סִפֵּק צָרְכֵּנוּ בַּמִּדְבָּר
אַרְבָּעִים שָׁנָה, דַּיֵּנוּ.

If He had just given us everything we needed
  in the desert for forty years,
  but not fed us the manna,
    it would have been enough for us!

אִלּוּ סִפֵּק צָרְכֵּנוּ בַּמִּדְבָּר
אַרְבָּעִים שָׁנָה,
וְלֹא הֶאֱכִילָנוּ אֶת הַמָּן, דַּיֵּנוּ.

If He had just fed us manna,
  but not given us the Sabbath,
    it would have been enough for us!

אִלּוּ הֶאֱכִילָנוּ אֶת הַמָּן,
וְלֹא נָתַן לָנוּ אֶת הַשַּׁבָּת, דַּיֵּנוּ.

If He had just given us the Sabbath,
but not brought us to Mount Sinai,
it would have been enough for us!
If He had just brought us to Mount Sinai,
but not given us the Torah,
it would have been enough for us!
If He had just given us the Torah,
but not brought us into *Eretz Yisrael*,
it would have been enough for us!
If He had just brought us into *Eretz Yisrael*,
but not built the *Bais Hamikdash* [Holy Temple]
for us,   it would have been enough for us!

אִלּוּ נָתַן לָנוּ אֶת הַשַּׁבָּת,
וְלֹא קֵרְבָנוּ לִפְנֵי הַר סִינַי,   דַּיֵּנוּ.

אִלּוּ קֵרְבָנוּ לִפְנֵי הַר סִינַי,
וְלֹא נָתַן לָנוּ אֶת הַתּוֹרָה,   דַּיֵּנוּ.

אִלּוּ נָתַן לָנוּ אֶת הַתּוֹרָה,
וְלֹא הִכְנִיסָנוּ לְאֶרֶץ יִשְׂרָאֵל,   דַּיֵּנוּ.

אִלּוּ הִכְנִיסָנוּ לְאֶרֶץ יִשְׂרָאֵל,
וְלֹא בָנָה לָנוּ אֶת בֵּית הַבְּחִירָה,   דַּיֵּנוּ.

Since God actually did so many great favors for us, we should be so much more grateful! (1) He took us out of Egypt, (2) punished the Egyptians, (3) destroyed their idols, (4) killed their firtborn, (5) gave us their wealth, (6) split the Sea for us, (7) brought us across it on dry land, (8) drowned our enemies in it, (9) gave us everything we needed in the desert for forty years, (10) fed us the manna, (11) gave us the Sabbath, (12) brought us to Mount Sinai, (13) gave us the Torah, (14) brought us into *Eretz Yisrael,* (15) and built the *Bais Hamikdash* for us — to bring us forgiveness for all our sins!

עַל אַחַת כַּמָּה, וְכַמָּה טוֹבָה כְפוּלָה וּמְכֻפֶּלֶת לַמָּקוֹם עָלֵינוּ. שֶׁהוֹצִיאָנוּ מִמִּצְרַיִם, וְעָשָׂה בָהֶם שְׁפָטִים, וְעָשָׂה בֵאלֹהֵיהֶם, וְהָרַג אֶת בְּכוֹרֵיהֶם, וְנָתַן לָנוּ אֶת מָמוֹנָם, וְקָרַע לָנוּ אֶת הַיָּם, וְהֶעֱבִירָנוּ בְתוֹכוֹ בֶּחָרָבָה, וְשִׁקַּע צָרֵינוּ בְּתוֹכוֹ, וְסִפֵּק צָרְכֵּנוּ בַּמִּדְבָּר אַרְבָּעִים שָׁנָה, וְהֶאֱכִילָנוּ אֶת הַמָּן, וְנָתַן לָנוּ אֶת הַשַּׁבָּת, וְקֵרְבָנוּ לִפְנֵי הַר סִינַי, וְנָתַן לָנוּ אֶת הַתּוֹרָה, וְהִכְנִיסָנוּ לְאֶרֶץ יִשְׂרָאֵל, וּבָנָה לָנוּ אֶת בֵּית הַבְּחִירָה, לְכַפֵּר עַל כָּל עֲוֹנוֹתֵינוּ.

אִלּוּ קֵרְבָנוּ לִפְנֵי הַר סִינַי ... — If He had just brought us to Mount Sinai ...

Why would we have been grateful if God had brought us to Mount Sinai but not given us the Torah? What was the purpose of going to Sinai if not for the Torah?

Someone who goes into a perfume factory comes out smelling sweet. It does not matter whether or not he buys anything. Just being in such a pleasant place leaves an effect. In the same way, we would have gained something at Mount Sinai even if we had not received the Torah. By being there, we felt, saw, and heard the holiness of God — and that alone had a great effect on us.

Rabban Gamliel used to say: Anyone who has not explained these three things on Pesach, has not fulfilled the *mitzvah* of the *Seder*. The three things are:

PESACH, MATZAH, and MARROR.

רַבָּן גַּמְלִיאֵל הָיָה אוֹמֵר. כָּל שֶׁלֹּא אָמַר שְׁלֹשָׁה דְּבָרִים אֵלּוּ בַּפֶּסַח, לֹא יָצָא יְדֵי חוֹבָתוֹ, וְאֵלוּ הֵן,

פֶּסַח. מַצָּה. וּמָרוֹר.

PESACH — Why did our ancestors eat an offering called *Pesach* when the *Bais Hamikdash* still stood? The word "Pesach" means "passed over" — so the Pesach offering reminds us that when God went from house to house to kill the Egyptian firstborn, He passed over the Jewish homes. As the Torah says: "You should tell your children, 'This is a Pesach offering to HASHEM because, when He killed the Egyptians, He passed over the homes of the Jewish people and He saved our families. In gratitude the Jewish people bowed and knelt.'"

פֶּסַח שֶׁהָיוּ אֲבוֹתֵינוּ אוֹכְלִים בִּזְמַן שֶׁבֵּית הַמִּקְדָּשׁ הָיָה קַיָּם, עַל שׁוּם מָה? עַל שׁוּם שֶׁפָּסַח הַקָּדוֹשׁ בָּרוּךְ הוּא עַל בָּתֵּי אֲבוֹתֵינוּ בְּמִצְרַיִם. שֶׁנֶּאֱמַר, וַאֲמַרְתֶּם, זֶבַח פֶּסַח הוּא לַיהוה, אֲשֶׁר פָּסַח עַל בָּתֵּי בְנֵי יִשְׂרָאֵל בְּמִצְרַיִם בְּנָגְפּוֹ אֶת מִצְרַיִם, וְאֶת בָּתֵּינוּ הִצִּיל, וַיִּקֹּד הָעָם וַיִּשְׁתַּחֲווּ.

פֶּסַח — Pesach.

The word פֶּסַח, *Pesach*, means "to pass over." In Egypt, God passed over the Jewish homes when He took the lives of the Egyptian firstborn. The plague struck every Egyptian family, but it passed over the Jews, even if they were surrounded on all sides by Egyptians.

There is another meaning also. Normally, people have to improve themselves step by step before they can deserve miracles. It takes a long time for people to do that. But in Egypt, God wanted to help the Jewish people so much that He did not wait for them to deserve His help. Instead, He passed over all those steps, and saved them from slavery, even before they deserved it.

This should give us hope at all times. Whenever the right time comes, God will show us great mercy, just as He did in Egypt.

Pick up or point to the matzah and say:

MATZAH — Why do we eat this matzah? Because God, the King of kings, showed us His glory and saved our ancestors by taking them from Egypt so quickly that there was no time for their dough to rise. As the Torah says: "They baked the dough they took from Egypt into matzos for it had not risen. They could not wait for the dough to rise because they were chased out of Egypt. And they had not prepared other food for the way."

מַצָּה זוֹ שֶׁאָנוּ אוֹכְלִים, עַל שׁוּם מָה? עַל שׁוּם שֶׁלֹּא הִסְפִּיק בְּצֵקָם שֶׁל אֲבוֹתֵינוּ לְהַחֲמִיץ, עַד שֶׁנִּגְלָה עֲלֵיהֶם מֶלֶךְ מַלְכֵי הַמְּלָכִים הַקָּדוֹשׁ בָּרוּךְ הוּא וּגְאָלָם. שֶׁנֶּאֱמַר, וַיֹּאפוּ אֶת הַבָּצֵק אֲשֶׁר הוֹצִיאוּ מִמִּצְרַיִם עֻגֹת מַצּוֹת כִּי לֹא חָמֵץ, כִּי גֹרְשׁוּ מִמִּצְרַיִם, וְלֹא יָכְלוּ לְהִתְמַהְמֵהַּ, וְגַם צֵדָה לֹא עָשׂוּ לָהֶם.

מַצָּה — Matzah.

Why didn't God tell the Jews to prepare food for their journey, so that they would have had time to bake bread?

The *Yetzer Hara* is our desire to commit sins and enjoy things that the Torah does not allow us to have. The Sages call the *Yetzer Hara* "שְׂאֹר שֶׁבְּעִסָּה, *the yeast in the dough.*" Just as yeast makes dough rise and become big and puffy, so our *Yetzer Hara* convinces us to act in ways that would make us haughty. Then it is easy for him to make us sin. People would be much less likely to do wrong if they would be satisfied with the simple things that they really need. In order to remind us of this, God made us leave Egypt so quickly that our dough did not have a chance to rise. This reminds us that the best way to be free is not to let ourselves become big and puffy with false pride.

Pick up or point to the *marror* and say:

מָרוֹר זֶה שֶׁאָנוּ אוֹכְלִים, עַל שׁוּם מָה? עַל שׁוּם שֶׁמֵּרְרוּ הַמִּצְרִים אֶת חַיֵּי אֲבוֹתֵינוּ בְּמִצְרָיִם. שֶׁנֶּאֱמַר, וַיְמָרְרוּ אֶת חַיֵּיהֶם, בַּעֲבֹדָה קָשָׁה, בְּחֹמֶר וּבִלְבֵנִים, וּבְכָל עֲבֹדָה בַּשָּׂדֶה, אֵת כָּל עֲבֹדָתָם אֲשֶׁר עָבְדוּ בָהֶם בְּפָרֶךְ.

MARROR — Why do we eat bitter vegetables? Because the Egyptians made our ancestors' lives bitter. As the Torah says: "The Egyptians made their lives bitter with hard work, with cement and bricks and all the work in the field. All the work they made them do was backbreaking labor."

מָרוֹר — Marror.

God told Jacob that He, God, would go down to Egypt together with the Jewish people and that He would leave the exile together with them. From this, our Sages learn, that even when we sin and are punished, God is with us and watches over us. Even the punishments are for our good — though we don't always understand why we are suffering. That is why we remember the bitterness of Egypt by eating *marror*. This is to remind us that even the bitter suffering of exile is part of God's plan to prepare us for the time when he will free us from our exile and bring us back to *Eretz Yisrael* to stay.

In every generation, each person must feel as if he personally had gone out of Egypt, as the Torah says: "You should tell your child on that day, 'When **I** left Egypt, HASHEM did miracles for **me** because of these *mitzvos.*' " God saved not only our ancestors, but also us along with them, as the Torah says: "And He took **us** out from there, in order to bring us to *Eretz Yisrael* and to give us the land that He promised to our ancestors."

בְּכָל דּוֹר וָדוֹר חַיָּב אָדָם לִרְאוֹת אֶת עַצְמוֹ כְּאִלּוּ הוּא יָצָא מִמִּצְרָיִם. שֶׁנֶּאֱמַר, וְהִגַּדְתָּ לְבִנְךָ בַּיּוֹם הַהוּא לֵאמֹר, בַּעֲבוּר זֶה עָשָׂה יהוה **לִי**, בְּצֵאתִי מִמִּצְרָיִם. לֹא אֶת אֲבוֹתֵינוּ בִּלְבָד גָּאַל הַקָּדוֹשׁ בָּרוּךְ הוּא, אֶלָּא אַף אֹתָנוּ גָּאַל עִמָּהֶם. שֶׁנֶּאֱמַר, **וְאוֹתָנוּ** הוֹצִיא מִשָּׁם, לְמַעַן הָבִיא אֹתָנוּ לָתֶת לָנוּ אֶת הָאָרֶץ אֲשֶׁר נִשְׁבַּע לַאֲבוֹתֵינוּ.

Cover the matzos. Each person picks up his wine cup and says joyously:

Because of all these miracles and favors that we have been telling about, it is our duty to give every kind of praise and blessing to the One Who did all these miracles for our ancestors and for us. He took us from slavery to freedom, from sadness to happiness, from mourning to celebration, from heavy darkness to great light, and from bondage to redemption! So let us sing a new song to Him — *Halleluyah!*

לְפִיכָךְ אֲנַחְנוּ חַיָּבִים לְהוֹדוֹת, לְהַלֵּל, לְשַׁבֵּחַ, לְפָאֵר, לְרוֹמֵם, לְהַדֵּר, לְבָרֵךְ, לְעַלֵּה, וּלְקַלֵּס, לְמִי שֶׁעָשָׂה לַאֲבוֹתֵינוּ וְלָנוּ אֶת כָּל הַנִּסִּים הָאֵלּוּ, הוֹצִיאָנוּ מֵעַבְדוּת לְחֵרוּת, מִיָּגוֹן לְשִׂמְחָה, וּמֵאֵבֶל לְיוֹם טוֹב, וּמֵאֲפֵלָה לְאוֹר גָּדוֹל, וּמִשִּׁעְבּוּד לִגְאֻלָּה, וְנֹאמַר לְפָנָיו שִׁירָה חֲדָשָׁה, הַלְלוּיָהּ.

In some families, the wine cups are put down and the matzos are uncovered.
In other families the matzos remain covered and the wine cups are held until they are drunk (p. 36).

*H*alleluyah! Give praise, you servants of HASHEM — give praise to HASHEM's Name! May HASHEM's Name be blessed forever. From the time the sun rises until it sets, HASHEM's Name is praised. HASHEM is above all the nations, His glory is above heaven. Who is like HASHEM our God Whose throne is so high? Yet, He lowers Himself to see what is happening on heaven and earth! He picks up a poor person from the dust; He raises a needy person from trash bins. He seats the poor person with princes, with the princes of his people. He changes a childless woman into a happy mother of children — *Halleluyah!*

הַלְלוּיָהּ הַלְלוּ עַבְדֵי יהוה, הַלְלוּ אֶת שֵׁם יהוה. יְהִי שֵׁם יהוה מְבֹרָךְ, מֵעַתָּה וְעַד עוֹלָם. מִמִּזְרַח שֶׁמֶשׁ עַד מְבוֹאוֹ, מְהֻלָּל שֵׁם יהוה. רָם עַל כָּל גּוֹיִם יהוה, עַל הַשָּׁמַיִם כְּבוֹדוֹ. מִי כַּיהוה אֱלֹהֵינוּ, הַמַּגְבִּיהִי לָשָׁבֶת. הַמַּשְׁפִּילִי לִרְאוֹת, בַּשָּׁמַיִם וּבָאָרֶץ. מְקִימִי מֵעָפָר דָּל, מֵאַשְׁפֹּת יָרִים אֶבְיוֹן. לְהוֹשִׁיבִי עִם נְדִיבִים, עִם נְדִיבֵי עַמּוֹ. מוֹשִׁיבִי עֲקֶרֶת הַבַּיִת, אֵם הַבָּנִים שְׂמֵחָה, הַלְלוּיָהּ.

הַלְלוּיָהּ — **Halleluyah.**
This familiar word is a combination of the two words הַלְלוּ יָהּ, *give praise to God.* When we say

Halleluyah, it is like we are calling out happily and excitedly to everyone that they should join us in praising God.

hen Israel left Egypt, when the Family of Jacob left a foreign people — Judah became God's holy nation, Israel became His loyal empire. When the Jews came to the Sea of Reeds, the Sea saw them and ran away; when they had to cross the Jordan River to enter *Eretz Yisrael*, the Jordan turned around and split. When God gave the Torah to Israel, the mountains danced like rams, the hills like little lambs. What happened to you, O Sea, that you ran away; O Jordan, that you turned around? You mountains, that you danced like rams, you hills, like little lambs? [They answer:] The whole world trembles before the Lord, before Jacob's God. When Israel needs water, He turns a rock into a pool of water, a hard rock into a spring of water!

בְּצֵאת יִשְׂרָאֵל מִמִּצְרָיִם, בֵּית יַעֲקֹב מֵעַם לֹעֵז. הָיְתָה יְהוּדָה לְקָדְשׁוֹ, יִשְׂרָאֵל מַמְשְׁלוֹתָיו. הַיָּם רָאָה וַיָּנֹס, הַיַּרְדֵּן יִסֹּב לְאָחוֹר. הֶהָרִים רָקְדוּ כְאֵילִים, גְּבָעוֹת כִּבְנֵי צֹאן. מַה לְּךָ הַיָּם כִּי תָנוּס, הַיַּרְדֵּן תִּסֹּב לְאָחוֹר. הֶהָרִים תִּרְקְדוּ כְאֵילִים, גְּבָעוֹת כִּבְנֵי צֹאן. מִלִּפְנֵי אָדוֹן חוּלִי אָרֶץ, מִלִּפְנֵי אֱלוֹהַּ יַעֲקֹב. הַהֹפְכִי הַצּוּר אֲגַם מָיִם, חַלָּמִישׁ לְמַעְיְנוֹ מָיִם.

Cover the matzos. Each person raises his wine cup and says the following blessing joyfully.
[On Saturday night, recite the phrase in brackets in place of the phrase before it.]

e bless You, HASHEM our God, King of the whole world, Who saved us and saved our ancestors from Egypt, and let us reach this night, to eat matzah and *marror*. In the same way, may HASHEM our God, the God of our fathers, bring us to future special times and holidays — may they come to us in peace — may we be gladdened by the rebuilding of Jerusalem and may we be joyful in serving You. In Jerusalem we will be able to eat from the offerings and from the Pesach offering [from the Pesach offering and the other offerings] whose blood will go on the wall of Your Altar, so that You will be pleased with us. And may we praise You with a new song for saving us and making our souls free. We bless You HASHEM, Who has saved Israel.

בָּרוּךְ אַתָּה יהוה אֱלֹהֵינוּ מֶלֶךְ הָעוֹלָם, אֲשֶׁר גְּאָלָנוּ וְגָאַל אֶת אֲבוֹתֵינוּ מִמִּצְרַיִם, וְהִגִּיעָנוּ הַלַּיְלָה הַזֶּה לֶאֱכָל בּוֹ מַצָּה וּמָרוֹר. כֵּן יהוה אֱלֹהֵינוּ וֵאלֹהֵי אֲבוֹתֵינוּ, יַגִּיעֵנוּ לְמוֹעֲדִים וְלִרְגָלִים אֲחֵרִים הַבָּאִים לִקְרָאתֵנוּ לְשָׁלוֹם, שְׂמֵחִים בְּבִנְיַן עִירֶךָ וְשָׂשִׂים בַּעֲבוֹדָתֶךָ, וְנֹאכַל שָׁם מִן הַזְּבָחִים וּמִן הַפְּסָחִים [מִן הַפְּסָחִים וּמִן הַזְּבָחִים] אֲשֶׁר יַגִּיעַ דָּמָם עַל קִיר מִזְבַּחֲךָ לְרָצוֹן. וְנוֹדֶה לְךָ שִׁיר חָדָשׁ עַל גְּאֻלָּתֵנוּ וְעַל פְּדוּת נַפְשֵׁנוּ. בָּרוּךְ אַתָּה יהוה, גָּאַל יִשְׂרָאֵל.

We bless You, HASHEM our God, King of the whole world, Who creates the fruit of the grapevine.

בָּרוּךְ אַתָּה יהוה אֱלֹהֵינוּ מֶלֶךְ הָעוֹלָם, בּוֹרֵא פְּרִי הַגָּפֶן.

Drink the wine immediately, while seated and reclining on the left side.

It is preferable to drink the entire cup, but at the very least, most of the cup.

The two parts of Hallel.

The first two chapters of *Hallel,* which we have just finished, are called הַלֵּל הַמִּצְרִי, the Egyptian *Hallel,* because they praise God for saving us from Egypt. Having finished this part of *Hallel,* we go to the *mitzvos* of matzah and *marror,* which remind us of that miracle. Then, after the meal, we go on to the second part of *Hallel,* which speaks of our hope for the coming of *Mashiach.*

By eating in the middle of *Hallel,* we show that even our meals are holy. During our *Seder* meal, we should continue to speak about God's miracles and praises. When a Jew eats with holiness, his meal becomes like a part of *Hallel.*

RACHTZAH

Wash your hands [pouring water from a cup, twice on the right hand and twice on the left] and recite the blessing. Except for the blessings, one should not speak until the matzos, *marror* and *korech* have been eaten.

We bless You, HASHEM our God, King of the whole world, Who made us holy with His mitzvos and commanded us to wash our hands.

בָּרוּךְ אַתָּה יהוה אֱלֹהֵינוּ מֶלֶךְ הָעוֹלָם, אֲשֶׁר קִדְּשָׁנוּ בְּמִצְוֹתָיו, וְצִוָּנוּ עַל נְטִילַת יָדַיִם.

MOTZI MATZAH

After all have washed and dried their hands, the father raises all three matzos and recites the first of the following two blessings:

We bless You, HASHEM our God, King of the whole world, Who brings bread out of the ground.

בָּרוּךְ אַתָּה יהוה אֱלֹהֵינוּ מֶלֶךְ הָעוֹלָם, הַמּוֹצִיא לֶחֶם מִן הָאָרֶץ.

(Others respond: אָמֵן, *Amen*)

The father puts down the bottom matzah and continues with the second blessing:

We bless You, HASHEM our God, King of the whole world, Who made us holy with His mitzvos and commanded us to eat matzah.

בָּרוּךְ אַתָּה יהוה אֱלֹהֵינוּ מֶלֶךְ הָעוֹלָם, אֲשֶׁר קִדְּשָׁנוּ בְּמִצְוֹתָיו, וְצִוָּנוּ עַל אֲכִילַת מַצָּה.

(Others respond: אָמֵן, *Amen*)

Each person is given a piece of each of the top two matzos. However, since everyone will receive only a small amount of matzah, there must be extra matzos at the table so that everyone can receive a substantial amount. Eat the matzah without delay, while seated and leaning on the left side.

MARROR

Marror reminds us of the bitterness of slavery. *Charoses* looks like mortar and reminds us of the hard labor. The *charoses* is made of food to which the Torah compares the Jewish people — apples, nuts, cinnamon, wine, etc. Each person is give a portion of *marror*. Dip the *marror* in *charoses*, then shake off the *charoses*. Recite the following blessing, keeping in mind that the blessing also applies to the כּוֹרֵךְ/Sandwich that will be eaten next.

We bless You, HASHEM our God, King of the whole world, who made us holy with His mitzvos and commanded us to eat bitter herbs.

בָּרוּךְ אַתָּה יהוה אֱלֹהֵינוּ מֶלֶךְ הָעוֹלָם, אֲשֶׁר קִדְּשָׁנוּ בְּמִצְוֹתָיו, וְצִוָּנוּ עַל אֲכִילַת מָרוֹר.

Eat the *marror* without delay. The *marror* is eaten without leaning.

KORECH

Each person is given a piece of the bottom matzah plus some additional matzah, and a second portion of *marror*. Dip the *marror* in *charoses*, then shake off the *charoses*. Put the matzah and *marror* together in the form of a sandwich, and recite the following paragraph:

his is a reminder of what Hillel used to do in the time of the *Bais Hamikdash*. When the *Bais Hamikdash* stood, Hillel used to combine matzah and *marror* in a sandwich and eat them together, doing as the Torah says: "They should eat the Pesach offering together with matzah and *marror*."

זֵכֶר לְמִקְדָּשׁ כְּהִלֵּל. כֵּן עָשָׂה הִלֵּל בִּזְמַן שֶׁבֵּית הַמִּקְדָּשׁ הָיָה קַיָּם. הָיָה כּוֹרֵךְ מַצָּה וּמָרוֹר וְאוֹכֵל בְּיַחַד. לְקַיֵּם מַה שֶׁנֶּאֱמַר, עַל מַצּוֹת וּמְרֹרִים יֹאכְלֻהוּ.

Eat the sandwich while leaning on the left side.

שֻׁלְחָן עוֹרֵךְ

SHULCHAN ORECH

The meal is part of the *Seder,* and should be eaten with the joy and respect that should accompany the performance of a *mitzvah.* One should be careful not to overeat, so that he will have an appetite for the *Afikoman.*

צָפוּן

TZAFUN

Each person is given a piece of the *Afikoman,* plus some additional matzah. It should be eaten while leaning on the left side, without delay, and preferably before midnight. After eating the *Afikoman,* one must not eat or drink anything except for the last two *Seder* wine cups (or water, tea, and the like).

אֲפִיקוֹמָן — Afikoman.

When the *Bais Hamikdash* stood and we had the *Pesach* offering, our Sages said that the last food eaten at the *Seder* should be the meat of the *Pesach,* so that the last taste in our mouths should be the *mitzvah*-food. Nowadays, we have no *Pesach* offering, but the eating of matzah is our special *mitzvah* of the *Seder.* The Sages want us to eat some matzah in place of the *Pesach,* so that we will have the taste of the matzah in our mouths for the rest of the night. We eat the *Afikoman* before midnight because that is the deadline for eating the *Pesach* offering. Since the *Afikoman* takes its place, we should finish eating it at the same time. The word *Afikoman* means "dessert." We call the matzah *Afikoman* because it is the last food we will eat at the *Seder* — just like dessert.

BARECH

Bircas Hamazon, Grace after Meals, is recited after each meal. It contains four blessings. The first was written by Moses when the manna fell; the second by Joshua when he led the nation into *Eretz Yisrael*; the third by David and Solomon when they built Jerusalem and the *Bais Hamikdash* [Holy Temple]; and the fourth by the court of Rabban Gamliel the Elder after the victims of the Roman massacre at Betar were brought to burial.

On the Sabbath and on holidays, we add appropriate paragraphs that speak of the holiness of the day.

THE THIRD CUP IS FILLED.

It is customary to recite the following psalm before *Bircas Hamazon*.

This is a song that the Levites used to sing as they walked up the steps of the *Bais Hamikdash* [Holy Temple]: When HASHEM sends Mashiach to bring us back to *Eretz Yisrael*, it will seem like a dream. Our mouths will be filled with happy laughter and our tongues will sing glad song. The gentile nations will exclaim, "What great things HASHEM has done for these Jews!" Yes — HASHEM will do great things for us, and we will rejoice. HASHEM — please bring back all the Jewish captives, and make us flourish like a desert that becomes full of flowing brooks. Let Your servants be like farmers who cry when they plant, but will sing for joy when they harvest their crops. Your servants will be like people who cry because they have only a few seeds to plant, but who will come back home joyously, carrying bundles of grain.

שִׁיר הַמַּעֲלוֹת, בְּשׁוּב יהוה אֶת שִׁיבַת צִיּוֹן, הָיִינוּ כְּחֹלְמִים. אָז יִמָּלֵא שְׂחוֹק פִּינוּ וּלְשׁוֹנֵנוּ רִנָּה, אָז יֹאמְרוּ בַגּוֹיִם, הִגְדִּיל יהוה לַעֲשׂוֹת עִם אֵלֶּה. הִגְדִּיל יהוה לַעֲשׂוֹת עִמָּנוּ, הָיִינוּ שְׂמֵחִים. שׁוּבָה יהוה אֶת שְׁבִיתֵנוּ, כַּאֲפִיקִים בַּנֶּגֶב. הַזֹּרְעִים בְּדִמְעָה בְּרִנָּה יִקְצֹרוּ. הָלוֹךְ יֵלֵךְ וּבָכֹה נֹשֵׂא מֶשֶׁךְ הַזָּרַע, בֹּא יָבֹא בְרִנָּה, נֹשֵׂא אֲלֻמֹּתָיו.

If three or more males, aged thirteen or older, participated in the meal, *Bircas Hamazon* is preceded by *zimun* — a formal invitation to recite the blessings together. If ten men or more join in the *zimun*, the words in brackets are added.

The leader begins:

Gentlemen, let us bless together.

רַבּוֹתַי נְבָרֵךְ.

The others respond:

Blessed is the Name of HASHEM, now and forever.

יְהִי שֵׁם יהוה מְבֹרָךְ מֵעַתָּה וְעַד עוֹלָם.

The leader continues:

Blessed is the Name of HASHEM, now and forever. With the permission of everyone here, let us bless Him [our God], Whose food we have eaten.

יְהִי שֵׁם יהוה מְבֹרָךְ מֵעַתָּה וְעַד עוֹלָם. בִּרְשׁוּת מָרָנָן וְרַבָּנָן וְרַבּוֹתַי נְבָרֵךְ [אֱלֹהֵינוּ] שֶׁאָכַלְנוּ מִשֶּׁלּוֹ.

The others respond:

We bless Him [our God] for we have eaten His food and we live through His goodness.

בָּרוּךְ [אֱלֹהֵינוּ] שֶׁאָכַלְנוּ מִשֶּׁלּוֹ וּבְטוּבוֹ חָיִינוּ.

The leader repeats:

We bless Him [our God] for we have eaten His food and we live through His goodness.

בָּרוּךְ [אֱלֹהֵינוּ] שֶׁאָכַלְנוּ מִשֶּׁלּוֹ וּבְטוּבוֹ חָיִינוּ.

[He is blessed and His Name is blessed.]

[בָּרוּךְ הוּא וּבָרוּךְ שְׁמוֹ.]

There are four blessings in *Bircas Hamazon*.
In the first blessing we thank God for giving us food.

e bless You, HASHEM our God, King of the whole world, Who feeds the entire world in His goodness — with love, kindness, and mercy. He gives food to all people, because His kindness lasts forever. Because of His great goodness, we have never lacked food; may He never let us lack food. Why do we ask for this? — so that we can praise His Great Name, because He is the merciful God, Who feeds and supports everyone, and does good to everyone, and Who prepares food for all His creatures that He has created. We bless You, HASHEM, Who feeds everyone.

בָּרוּךְ אַתָּה יהוה אֱלֹהֵינוּ מֶלֶךְ הָעוֹלָם, הַזָּן אֶת הָעוֹלָם כֻּלּוֹ, בְּטוּבוֹ, בְּחֵן בְּחֶסֶד וּבְרַחֲמִים. הוּא נֹתֵן לֶחֶם לְכָל בָּשָׂר, כִּי לְעוֹלָם חַסְדּוֹ. וּבְטוּבוֹ הַגָּדוֹל, תָּמִיד לֹא חָסַר לָנוּ, וְאַל יֶחְסַר לָנוּ, מָזוֹן לְעוֹלָם וָעֶד. בַּעֲבוּר שְׁמוֹ הַגָּדוֹל, כִּי הוּא אֵל זָן וּמְפַרְנֵס לַכֹּל, וּמֵטִיב לַכֹּל, וּמֵכִין מָזוֹן לְכָל בְּרִיּוֹתָיו אֲשֶׁר בָּרָא. בָּרוּךְ אַתָּה יהוה, הַזָּן אֶת הַכֹּל.

In the second blessing we thank God for giving us *Eretz Yisrael*.

e thank You for many things, HASHEM our God: for giving Eretz Yisrael to our ancestors as our own land — a fine, good, broad land; for taking us out of Egypt and saving us from slavery; for the *mitzvah* of *bris milah*; for the Torah that You taught us; for the *mitzvos* that You made known to us; for the life, love, and kindness that You graciously gave us; for the food with which You always feed and support us every day, every season, and every hour.

נוֹדֶה לְךָ יהוה אֱלֹהֵינוּ, עַל שֶׁהִנְחַלְתָּ לַאֲבוֹתֵינוּ אֶרֶץ חֶמְדָּה טוֹבָה וּרְחָבָה. וְעַל שֶׁהוֹצֵאתָנוּ יהוה אֱלֹהֵינוּ מֵאֶרֶץ מִצְרַיִם וּפְדִיתָנוּ מִבֵּית עֲבָדִים, וְעַל בְּרִיתְךָ שֶׁחָתַמְתָּ בִּבְשָׂרֵנוּ, וְעַל תּוֹרָתְךָ שֶׁלִּמַּדְתָּנוּ, וְעַל חֻקֶּיךָ שֶׁהוֹדַעְתָּנוּ, וְעַל חַיִּים חֵן וָחֶסֶד שֶׁחוֹנַנְתָּנוּ, וְעַל אֲכִילַת מָזוֹן שָׁאַתָּה זָן וּמְפַרְנֵס אוֹתָנוּ תָּמִיד, בְּכָל יוֹם וּבְכָל עֵת וּבְכָל שָׁעָה.

or all this we thank You and bless You, HASHEM, our God. May Your Name always be blessed by everyone forever, as it is written in the Torah: "You will eat and be satisfied, and then you will bless HASHEM your God for the good land that He gave you." We bless You, HASHEM, for the Land and for the food.

וְעַל הַכֹּל יהוה אֱלֹהֵינוּ אֲנַחְנוּ מוֹדִים לָךְ, וּמְבָרְכִים אוֹתָךְ, יִתְבָּרַךְ שִׁמְךָ בְּפִי כָּל חַי תָּמִיד לְעוֹלָם וָעֶד. כַּכָּתוּב, וְאָכַלְתָּ וְשָׂבָעְתָּ, וּבֵרַכְתָּ אֶת יהוה אֱלֹהֶיךָ, עַל הָאָרֶץ הַטֹּבָה אֲשֶׁר נָתַן לָךְ. בָּרוּךְ אַתָּה יהוה, עַל הָאָרֶץ וְעַל הַמָּזוֹן.

In the third blessing we pray for the rebuilding of Jerusalem.

Have mercy, HASHEM our God, on Israel, Your people; on Jerusalem, Your city; on the Temple Mount, the place of Your Glory; on the kingdom of the family of David, Your anointed king; and on the great and holy *Bais Hamikdash,* which is called by Your Name. O God, our Father — take care of us, feed us, support us, supply our needs, and make our lives easier. HASHEM our God, give us speedy relief from all our troubles. Please, HASHEM our God, don't make us need the gifts or loans of other people; let us get all our needs only from Your hand, which is full, open, holy, and generous. Then we will never feel ashamed or be embarrassed.

רַחֵם (נָא) יהוה אֱלֹהֵינוּ עַל יִשְׂרָאֵל עַמֶּךָ, וְעַל יְרוּשָׁלַיִם עִירֶךָ, וְעַל צִיּוֹן מִשְׁכַּן כְּבוֹדֶךָ, וְעַל מַלְכוּת בֵּית דָּוִד מְשִׁיחֶךָ, וְעַל הַבַּיִת הַגָּדוֹל וְהַקָּדוֹשׁ שֶׁנִּקְרָא שִׁמְךָ עָלָיו. אֱלֹהֵינוּ אָבִינוּ רְעֵנוּ זוּנֵנוּ פַּרְנְסֵנוּ וְכַלְכְּלֵנוּ וְהַרְוִיחֵנוּ, וְהַרְוַח לָנוּ יהוה אֱלֹהֵינוּ מְהֵרָה מִכָּל צָרוֹתֵינוּ. וְנָא אַל תַּצְרִיכֵנוּ יהוה אֱלֹהֵינוּ, לֹא לִידֵי מַתְּנַת בָּשָׂר וָדָם, וְלֹא לִידֵי הַלְוָאָתָם, כִּי אִם לְיָדְךָ הַמְּלֵאָה הַפְּתוּחָה הַקְּדוֹשָׁה וְהָרְחָבָה, שֶׁלֹּא נֵבוֹשׁ וְלֹא נִכָּלֵם לְעוֹלָם וָעֶד.

On the Sabbath recite this paragraph:

May it please You, HASHEM our God, to make us healthy through Your *mitzvos* and through the *mitzvah* of this great and holy Shabbos. Because to You, this is a great and holy day, to rest on it and be calm on it lovingly, as You have commanded us. Please, HASHEM our God, let us be calm, so that there will not be trouble, sadness, or moaning on this day of our rest. HASHEM our God, let us see Zion, Your city, being comforted, and Jerusalem, city of Your holiness, being rebuilt — because only You have the power to help and to comfort.

רְצֵה וְהַחֲלִיצֵנוּ יהוה אֱלֹהֵינוּ בְּמִצְוֹתֶיךָ, וּבְמִצְוַת יוֹם הַשְּׁבִיעִי הַשַּׁבָּת הַגָּדוֹל וְהַקָּדוֹשׁ הַזֶּה, כִּי יוֹם זֶה גָּדוֹל וְקָדוֹשׁ הוּא לְפָנֶיךָ, לִשְׁבָּת בּוֹ וְלָנוּחַ בּוֹ בְּאַהֲבָה כְּמִצְוַת רְצוֹנֶךָ, וּבִרְצוֹנְךָ הָנִיחַ לָנוּ יהוה אֱלֹהֵינוּ, שֶׁלֹּא תְהֵא צָרָה וְיָגוֹן וַאֲנָחָה בְּיוֹם מְנוּחָתֵנוּ, וְהַרְאֵנוּ יהוה אֱלֹהֵינוּ בְּנֶחָמַת צִיּוֹן עִירֶךָ, וּבְבִנְיַן יְרוּשָׁלַיִם עִיר קָדְשֶׁךָ, כִּי אַתָּה הוּא בַּעַל הַיְשׁוּעוֹת וּבַעַל הַנֶּחָמוֹת.

Our God and the God of our forefathers, we beg that the following thoughts rise, come to You, reach You, be seen, be pleasing, be heard, be considered, and be remembered. The thoughts are: memories of ourselves; memories of our ancestors; of *Mashiach,* the descendant of Your servant David; of Jerusalem, Your Holy City; and of Your entire nation, the Family of Israel. May You think of all these things to save us all and to be good, gracious, kind and merciful to us, to give us life and peace on this day of the *Yom Tov* of Matzos. Remember us today, HASHEM our God, for good; think about us for blessing; and help us to have a good life. And regarding help and mercy — please have pity, be gracious, be merciful, and save us, because we look to You for help, since You are the generous and merciful God.

אֱלֹהֵינוּ וֵאלֹהֵי אֲבוֹתֵינוּ, יַעֲלֶה, וְיָבֹא, וְיַגִּיעַ, וְיֵרָאֶה, וְיֵרָצֶה, וְיִשָּׁמַע, וְיִפָּקֵד, וְיִזָּכֵר, זִכְרוֹנֵנוּ וּפִקְדוֹנֵנוּ, וְזִכְרוֹן אֲבוֹתֵינוּ, וְזִכְרוֹן מָשִׁיחַ בֶּן דָּוִד עַבְדֶּךָ, וְזִכְרוֹן יְרוּשָׁלַיִם עִיר קָדְשֶׁךָ, וְזִכְרוֹן כָּל עַמְּךָ בֵּית יִשְׂרָאֵל לְפָנֶיךָ, לִפְלֵיטָה לְטוֹבָה לְחֵן וּלְחֶסֶד וּלְרַחֲמִים, לְחַיִּים וּלְשָׁלוֹם בְּיוֹם חַג הַמַּצּוֹת הַזֶּה. זָכְרֵנוּ יהוה אֱלֹהֵינוּ בּוֹ לְטוֹבָה, וּפָקְדֵנוּ בוֹ לִבְרָכָה, וְהוֹשִׁיעֵנוּ בוֹ לְחַיִּים (טוֹבִים). וּבִדְבַר יְשׁוּעָה וְרַחֲמִים חוּס וְחָנֵּנוּ וְרַחֵם עָלֵינוּ וְהוֹשִׁיעֵנוּ, כִּי אֵלֶיךָ עֵינֵינוּ, כִּי אֵל חַנּוּן וְרַחוּם אָתָּה.

May You rebuild Jerusalem, the Holy City, soon in our lifetime. We bless You, HASHEM, Who rebuilds Jerusalem in His mercy. Amen.

וּבְנֵה יְרוּשָׁלַיִם עִיר הַקֹּדֶשׁ בִּמְהֵרָה בְיָמֵינוּ. בָּרוּךְ אַתָּה יהוה, בּוֹנֵה בְרַחֲמָיו יְרוּשָׁלָיִם. אָמֵן.

In the fourth blessing we thank God for His goodness.

We bless You, HASHEM our God, King of the whole world, the Almighty, our Father, our King, our Master, our Creator, our Redeemer, our Maker; our Holy One, the Holy One of Jacob; our Shepherd, the Shepherd of Israel; He is the King Who is good and Who does good to everyone. Every single day, He did good, He does good, and He will do good for us. He gave us very much, He gives us very much and He will give us very much forever — with love, kindness, and mercy; giving us relief through rescue, success, blessing, help, comfort, livelihood, support, mercy, life, peace, and all good things. May He never keep us from having all good things.

בָּרוּךְ אַתָּה יהוה אֱלֹהֵינוּ מֶלֶךְ הָעוֹלָם, הָאֵל אָבִינוּ מַלְכֵּנוּ אַדִּירֵנוּ בּוֹרְאֵנוּ גּוֹאֲלֵנוּ יוֹצְרֵנוּ קְדוֹשֵׁנוּ קְדוֹשׁ יַעֲקֹב, רוֹעֵנוּ רוֹעֵה יִשְׂרָאֵל, הַמֶּלֶךְ הַטּוֹב וְהַמֵּטִיב לַכֹּל, שֶׁבְּכָל יוֹם וָיוֹם הוּא הֵטִיב, הוּא מֵטִיב, הוּא יֵיטִיב לָנוּ. הוּא גְמָלָנוּ, הוּא גוֹמְלֵנוּ, הוּא יִגְמְלֵנוּ לָעַד, לְחֵן וּלְחֶסֶד וּלְרַחֲמִים וּלְרֶוַח הַצָּלָה וְהַצְלָחָה, בְּרָכָה וִישׁוּעָה נֶחָמָה פַּרְנָסָה וְכַלְכָּלָה וְרַחֲמִים וְחַיִּים וְשָׁלוֹם וְכָל טוֹב, וּמִכָּל טוּב לְעוֹלָם אַל יְחַסְּרֵנוּ.

May the Merciful God always be our King. May the Merciful God be blessed in heaven and on earth.

May the Merciful God be praised in every generation; and may He always be proud of us and forever be honored by the way we act.

May the Merciful God support us with honor.

May the Merciful God break the yoke of suffering that is on our neck and may He lead us proudly to our land.

May the Merciful God send us much blessing in this house and on this table where we have eaten.

May the Merciful God send us Elijah the Prophet, who is remembered for doing good, to bring us good news, to save us and comfort us.

הָרַחֲמָן הוּא יִמְלוֹךְ עָלֵינוּ לְעוֹלָם וָעֶד. הָרַחֲמָן הוּא יִתְבָּרַךְ בַּשָּׁמַיִם וּבָאָרֶץ. הָרַחֲמָן הוּא יִשְׁתַּבַּח לְדוֹר דּוֹרִים, וְיִתְפָּאַר בָּנוּ לָעַד וּלְנֵצַח נְצָחִים, וְיִתְהַדַּר בָּנוּ לָעַד וּלְעוֹלְמֵי עוֹלָמִים. הָרַחֲמָן הוּא יְפַרְנְסֵנוּ בְּכָבוֹד. הָרַחֲמָן הוּא יִשְׁבּוֹר עֻלֵּנוּ מֵעַל צַוָּארֵנוּ, וְהוּא יוֹלִיכֵנוּ קוֹמְמִיּוּת לְאַרְצֵנוּ. הָרַחֲמָן הוּא יִשְׁלַח לָנוּ בְּרָכָה מְרֻבָּה בַּבַּיִת הַזֶּה, וְעַל שֻׁלְחָן זֶה שֶׁאָכַלְנוּ עָלָיו. הָרַחֲמָן הוּא יִשְׁלַח לָנוּ אֶת אֵלִיָּהוּ הַנָּבִיא זָכוּר לַטּוֹב, וִיבַשֶּׂר לָנוּ בְּשׂוֹרוֹת טוֹבוֹת יְשׁוּעוֹת וְנֶחָמוֹת.

ay it be God's will that this host not be shamed nor embarrassed either in This World or in the World to Come. May he succeed in all his dealings. May his dealings be successful and convenient. May no evil rule over his work, and may no sin or evil thought attach itself to him, from now and forever.

יְהִי רָצוֹן, שֶׁלֹּא יֵבוֹשׁ וְלֹא יִכָּלֵם בַּעַל הַבַּיִת הַזֶּה, לֹא בָּעוֹלָם הַזֶּה, וְלֹא בָּעוֹלָם הַבָּא. וְיַצְלִיחַ בְּכָל נְכָסָיו, וְיִהְיוּ נְכָסָיו מוּצְלָחִים וּקְרוֹבִים לָעִיר. וְאַל יִשְׁלוֹט שָׂטָן בְּמַעֲשֵׂה יָדָיו, וְאַל יִזְדַּקֵּק לְפָנָיו שׁוּם דְּבַר חֵטְא וְהִרְהוּר עָוֹן, מֵעַתָּה וְעַד עוֹלָם.

Someone eating at his own table recites the following
and includes the words in parentheses that apply.

May the Merciful God bless me (and my wife/husband and my children) and all that is mine,

הָרַחֲמָן הוּא יְבָרֵךְ אוֹתִי (וְאֶת אִשְׁתִּי/בַּעֲלִי. וְאֶת זַרְעִי) וְאֶת כָּל אֲשֶׁר לִי.

Someone eating at another's table recites the following.
Children at their parents' table add the words in parentheses.

May the Merciful God bless (my father and teacher) the head of this house, and (my mother and teacher) lady of this house — may He bless them, their home, their children and everything they have,

הָרַחֲמָן הוּא יְבָרֵךְ אֶת (אָבִי מוֹרִי) בַּעַל הַבַּיִת הַזֶּה, וְאֶת (אִמִּי מוֹרָתִי) בַּעֲלַת הַבַּיִת הַזֶּה. אוֹתָם וְאֶת בֵּיתָם וְאֶת זַרְעָם וְאֶת כָּל אֲשֶׁר לָהֶם.

All continue here:

us and everything that we have — just as our forefathers Abraham, Isaac, and Jacob were blessed in everything, from everything, and with everything. In the same way may He give all of us together a perfect blessing. Let us say: Amen!

אוֹתָנוּ וְאֶת כָּל אֲשֶׁר לָנוּ, כְּמוֹ שֶׁנִּתְבָּרְכוּ אֲבוֹתֵינוּ אַבְרָהָם יִצְחָק וְיַעֲקֹב בַּכֹּל מִכֹּל כֹּל, כֵּן יְבָרֵךְ אוֹתָנוּ כֻּלָּנוּ יַחַד בִּבְרָכָה שְׁלֵמָה. וְנֹאמַר, אָמֵן.

 n Heaven above, may both they and we be found deserving of peace. May we get a blessing from HASHEM and charity from God Who saves us, and may our acts be considered loving and wise by God and by people.

בַּמָּרוֹם יְלַמְּדוּ עֲלֵיהֶם וְעָלֵינוּ זְכוּת, שֶׁתְּהֵא לְמִשְׁמֶרֶת שָׁלוֹם. וְנִשָּׂא בְרָכָה מֵאֵת יהוה, וּצְדָקָה מֵאֱלֹהֵי יִשְׁעֵנוּ, וְנִמְצָא חֵן וְשֵׂכֶל טוֹב בְּעֵינֵי אֱלֹהִים וְאָדָם.

On the Sabbath recite this paragraph:	
May the Merciful God let us inherit the Shabbos of the World to Come, which will be a complete rest day forever.	הָרַחֲמָן הוּא יַנְחִילֵנוּ יוֹם שֶׁכֻּלּוֹ שַׁבָּת וּמְנוּחָה לְחַיֵּי הָעוֹלָמִים.

At the Seder recite the words in parentheses:

 ay the Merciful God let us inherit the day that is completely good (the day that lasts forever, the day when righteous people will sit with crowns on their heads and enjoy the glow of God's Presence — and may we be among them).

הָרַחֲמָן הוּא יַנְחִילֵנוּ יוֹם שֶׁכֻּלּוֹ טוֹב. (יוֹם שֶׁכֻּלּוֹ אָרוּךְ. יוֹם שֶׁצַּדִּיקִים יוֹשְׁבִים וְעַטְרוֹתֵיהֶם בְּרָאשֵׁיהֶם וְנֶהֱנִים מִזִּיו הַשְּׁכִינָה, וִיהִי חֶלְקֵנוּ עִמָּהֶם.)

ay the Merciful God give us the honor of living until the days of *Mashiach* and the life of the World to Come. God is a tower of help to His king and shows kindness to His anointed one, to David and his children, forever. Just as God makes peace in His heaven, may He also bring peace upon us and upon all Jews. Now answer: Amen.

הָרַחֲמָן הוּא יְזַכֵּנוּ לִימוֹת הַמָּשִׁיחַ וּלְחַיֵּי הָעוֹלָם הַבָּא. מִגְדּוֹל יְשׁוּעוֹת מַלְכּוֹ, וְעֹשֶׂה חֶסֶד לִמְשִׁיחוֹ, לְדָוִד וּלְזַרְעוֹ עַד עוֹלָם. עֹשֶׂה שָׁלוֹם בִּמְרוֹמָיו, הוּא יַעֲשֶׂה שָׁלוֹם עָלֵינוּ, וְעַל כָּל יִשְׂרָאֵל. וְאִמְרוּ, אָמֵן.

ou holy people of HASHEM — you should fear HASHEM, because those who fear Him do not lack anything. Even strong young lions may go hungry, but those who try to be close to HASHEM will not be missing anything that is good. Give thanks to HASHEM for He is good, because His kindness lasts forever. O God — You open Your hand and give every living thing what it desires. Blessed is the person who trusts HASHEM — then HASHEM will protect him. I was young and I became old, but I never saw a righteous person who was all alone and whose children had to beg for bread. HASHEM will give strength to His nation, HASHEM will bless His nation with peace.

יְראוּ אֶת יהוה קְדֹשָׁיו, כִּי אֵין מַחְסוֹר לִירֵאָיו. כְּפִירִים רָשׁוּ וְרָעֵבוּ, וְדֹרְשֵׁי יהוה לֹא יַחְסְרוּ כָל טוֹב. הוֹדוּ לַיהוה כִּי טוֹב, כִּי לְעוֹלָם חַסְדּוֹ. פּוֹתֵחַ אֶת יָדֶךָ, וּמַשְׂבִּיעַ לְכָל חַי רָצוֹן. בָּרוּךְ הַגֶּבֶר אֲשֶׁר יִבְטַח בַּיהוה, וְהָיָה יהוה מִבְטַחוֹ. נַעַר הָיִיתִי גַּם זָקַנְתִּי, וְלֹא רָאִיתִי צַדִּיק נֶעֱזָב, וְזַרְעוֹ מְבַקֶּשׁ לָחֶם. יהוה עֹז לְעַמּוֹ יִתֵּן, יהוה יְבָרֵךְ אֶת עַמּוֹ בַשָּׁלוֹם.

Raise the cup and recite the blessing:

We bless You, HASHEM our God, King of the whole world, Who creates the fruit of the grapevine.

Drink the wine immediately, while seated and reclining on the left side.

בָּרוּךְ אַתָּה יהוה אֱלֹהֵינוּ מֶלֶךְ הָעוֹלָם, בּוֹרֵא פְּרִי הַגָּפֶן.

It is preferable to drink the entire cup, but at the very least, most of the cup.

בִּרְכַּת הַמָּזוֹן — **Bircas Hamazon.**

When God gave מָן, *manna,* to our forefathers in the wilderness, Moses composed a blessing to thank Him. We still use Moses' blessing — it is the first paragraph of *Bircas Hamazon*. When we think of that fact, it reminds us of a very important lesson.

In the desert, our forefathers ate food that came down from heaven every morning. Everyone knew that God was giving him his daily food, and that he would starve without God's mercy. Nowadays, when we work hard to produce our food, or to earn money with which to buy it, it is easy for us to forget that it all comes from God. But when we recite Moses' blessing, it reminds us that whether we eat manna or food grown on our farms or prepared in our kitchen — everything comes from God.

וְלֹא רָאִיתִי צַדִּיק נֶעֱזָב — **I never saw a righteous person who was all alone.**

How can we say that we have never seen a *tzaddik* who is all alone? Haven't we all seen good people who are poor or who suffer?

Of course we have. This verse has a few meanings. Since a *tzaddik* knows that everything comes from God and that He is always merciful, the *tzaddik* never *feels* alone — because he has faith that God has done it all for a good reason.

There is another way to explain this verse. A Jewish person should never feel all alone because Jews always help one another. Even if someone does not have a penny to his name, the rest of us rush to help him. How can any Jew feel comfortable if his neighbor is going hungry?

THE FOURTH CUP IS FILLED.

An extra cup is filled in honor of Elijah the Prophet.

The front door of the house is opened to show that Pesach
is לֵיל שִׁמּוּרִים, a night when God protects us against danger.

שְׁפֹךְ חֲמָתְךָ אֶל הַגּוֹיִם אֲשֶׁר לֹא
יְדָעוּךָ, וְעַל מַמְלָכוֹת אֲשֶׁר
בְּשִׁמְךָ לֹא קָרָאוּ. כִּי אָכַל אֶת יַעֲקֹב,
וְאֶת נָוֵהוּ הֵשַׁמּוּ. שְׁפָךְ עֲלֵיהֶם זַעֲמֶךָ,
וַחֲרוֹן אַפְּךָ יַשִּׂיגֵם. תִּרְדֹּף בְּאַף,
וְתַשְׁמִידֵם מִתַּחַת שְׁמֵי יהוה.

God — Pour Your anger on the nations that do not want to know You and on the kingdoms that do not pray to You. For they tried to ruin the Jewish people and they destroyed the *Bais Hamikdash*. Pour Your annoyance on them and let Your burning anger catch them. Chase them with rage and destroy them from under HASHEM's heaven.

The door is closed.

HALLEL

The first two paragraphs of *Hallel* were recited before the meal. We now recite the rest of *Hallel* and other praises.

H ASHEM, do not give us honor for our own sake — give honor to Your Name, so that everyone will know You are kind and true. Why should the nations say, "Where is their God?" — Our God is in heaven and does whatever He wants! Their idols are silver and gold — they are made by people. They have a mouth, but they cannot speak; they have eyes, but they cannot see. They have ears, but they cannot hear; they have a nose, but they cannot smell. Their hands cannot feel, their feet cannot walk, they cannot make a sound from their throats. Those who make idols and everyone who believes in them should become like them! O Jewish People, rely on HASHEM — He is the help and shield of those who trust Him! O *Kohanim,* rely on HASHEM — He is the help and shield of those who trust Him! Those who fear HASHEM, rely on HASHEM — He is the help and shield of those who trust Him!

H ASHEM Who has remembered us will give blessing; He will bless the Family of Israel, He will bless the Family of Aaron. He will bless God-fearing people, the small and the great. May HASHEM give more and more to you and your children. You are blessed by HASHEM, Who makes heaven and earth. The heavens must obey HASHEM, but He gave the earth to people, who decide for themselves how they will act. Wicked people who deserve to die do not praise God, they are like those lowered into the silent grave. But we who are alive will bless God from now and forever, *Halleluyah!*

לֹא לָנוּ יהוה לֹא לָנוּ, כִּי לְשִׁמְךָ תֵּן כָּבוֹד, עַל חַסְדְּךָ עַל אֲמִתֶּךָ. לָמָּה יֹאמְרוּ הַגּוֹיִם, אַיֵּה נָא אֱלֹהֵיהֶם. וֵאלֹהֵינוּ בַשָּׁמַיִם, כֹּל אֲשֶׁר חָפֵץ עָשָׂה. עֲצַבֵּיהֶם כֶּסֶף וְזָהָב, מַעֲשֵׂה יְדֵי אָדָם. פֶּה לָהֶם וְלֹא יְדַבֵּרוּ, עֵינַיִם לָהֶם וְלֹא יִרְאוּ. אָזְנַיִם לָהֶם וְלֹא יִשְׁמָעוּ, אַף לָהֶם וְלֹא יְרִיחוּן. יְדֵיהֶם וְלֹא יְמִישׁוּן, רַגְלֵיהֶם וְלֹא יְהַלֵּכוּ, לֹא יֶהְגּוּ בִּגְרוֹנָם. כְּמוֹהֶם יִהְיוּ עֹשֵׂיהֶם כֹּל אֲשֶׁר בֹּטֵחַ בָּהֶם. יִשְׂרָאֵל בְּטַח בַּיהוה, עֶזְרָם וּמָגִנָּם הוּא. בֵּית אַהֲרֹן בִּטְחוּ בַיהוה, עֶזְרָם וּמָגִנָּם הוּא. יִרְאֵי יהוה בִּטְחוּ בַיהוה, עֶזְרָם וּמָגִנָּם הוּא.

יהוה זְכָרָנוּ יְבָרֵךְ, יְבָרֵךְ אֶת בֵּית יִשְׂרָאֵל, יְבָרֵךְ אֶת בֵּית אַהֲרֹן. יְבָרֵךְ יִרְאֵי יהוה, הַקְּטַנִּים עִם הַגְּדֹלִים. יֹסֵף יהוה עֲלֵיכֶם, עֲלֵיכֶם וְעַל בְּנֵיכֶם. בְּרוּכִים אַתֶּם לַיהוה, עֹשֵׂה שָׁמַיִם וָאָרֶץ. הַשָּׁמַיִם שָׁמַיִם לַיהוה, וְהָאָרֶץ נָתַן לִבְנֵי אָדָם. לֹא הַמֵּתִים יְהַלְלוּ יָהּ, וְלֹא כָּל יֹרְדֵי דוּמָה. וַאֲנַחְנוּ נְבָרֵךְ יָהּ, מֵעַתָּה וְעַד עוֹלָם, הַלְלוּיָהּ.

I love HASHEM because He hears my prayers. He turns His ear to me, so I will pray to Him as long as I live. I am surrounded by murderous enemies, the grave closes in on me — I discovered trouble and sadness. Then I call out HASHEM's Name and say, "Please, HASHEM, save my life!" HASHEM is generous and righteous, and our God is merciful. HASHEM protects foolish people, when I fall down He will save me. My soul — you will find peace again because HASHEM will be generous to you. [I say to God] "You have saved my soul from death and my eyes from tears, my feet from tripping." I wish I could walk before HASHEM in *Eretz Yisrael.* I believed in God even when I would say, "I suffer very much." Even when I [King David] was rushing to escape my enemies, I trusted so strongly in God that I declared, "Every one who says I will not become king is a liar!"

How can I repay HASHEM for all the good things He did for me? I will raise a cup of wine to thank and praise HASHEM for saving me. In front of His entire nation, I will bring to HASHEM the offerings that I promised Him. HASHEM does not like to see the death of those who are loyal to Him. Please, HASHEM — because I am Your servant and my mother was Your maid, I will thank You for making me free. I will bring You an offering of thanksgiving and I will pray to Your Name. In front of His entire nation, I will bring to HASHEM the offerings that I promised Him. In the courtyards of the *Bais Hamikdash,* in the middle of Jerusalem, *Halleluyah!*

Praise HASHEM, all you nations; praise Him, all you countries. You should do so because His kindness to us was so great, and HASHEM's promise stays true forever. *Halleluyah!*

Give thanks to HASHEM for He is good,
    His kindness lasts forever!
Let Israel say, His kindness lasts forever!
Let the House of Aaron say,
    His kindness lasts forever!
Let the God-fearing people say,
    His kindness lasts forever!

אָהַבְתִּי כִּי יִשְׁמַע יהוה, אֶת קוֹלִי תַּחֲנוּנָי. כִּי הִטָּה אָזְנוֹ לִי, וּבְיָמַי אֶקְרָא. אֲפָפוּנִי חֶבְלֵי מָוֶת, וּמְצָרֵי שְׁאוֹל מְצָאוּנִי, צָרָה וְיָגוֹן אֶמְצָא. וּבְשֵׁם יהוה אֶקְרָא, אָנָּה יהוה מַלְּטָה נַפְשִׁי. חַנּוּן יהוה וְצַדִּיק, וֵאלֹהֵינוּ מְרַחֵם. שֹׁמֵר פְּתָאִים יהוה, דַּלּוֹתִי וְלִי יְהוֹשִׁיעַ. שׁוּבִי נַפְשִׁי לִמְנוּחָיְכִי, כִּי יהוה גָּמַל עָלָיְכִי. כִּי חִלַּצְתָּ נַפְשִׁי מִמָּוֶת אֶת עֵינִי מִן דִּמְעָה, אֶת רַגְלִי מִדֶּחִי. אֶתְהַלֵּךְ לִפְנֵי יהוה, בְּאַרְצוֹת הַחַיִּים. הֶאֱמַנְתִּי כִּי אֲדַבֵּר, אֲנִי עָנִיתִי מְאֹד. אֲנִי אָמַרְתִּי בְחָפְזִי, כָּל הָאָדָם כֹּזֵב.

מָה אָשִׁיב לַיהוה, כָּל תַּגְמוּלוֹהִי עָלָי. כּוֹס יְשׁוּעוֹת אֶשָּׂא, וּבְשֵׁם יהוה אֶקְרָא. נְדָרַי לַיהוה אֲשַׁלֵּם, נֶגְדָה נָא לְכָל עַמּוֹ. יָקָר בְּעֵינֵי יהוה, הַמָּוְתָה לַחֲסִידָיו. אָנָּה יהוה כִּי אֲנִי עַבְדֶּךָ, אֲנִי עַבְדְּךָ, בֶּן אֲמָתֶךָ, פִּתַּחְתָּ לְמוֹסֵרָי. לְךָ אֶזְבַּח זֶבַח תּוֹדָה, וּבְשֵׁם יהוה אֶקְרָא. נְדָרַי לַיהוה אֲשַׁלֵּם, נֶגְדָה נָא לְכָל עַמּוֹ. בְּחַצְרוֹת בֵּית יהוה, בְּתוֹכֵכִי יְרוּשָׁלָיִם הַלְלוּיָהּ.

הַלְלוּ אֶת יהוה, כָּל גּוֹיִם, שַׁבְּחוּהוּ כָּל הָאֻמִּים. כִּי גָבַר עָלֵינוּ חַסְדּוֹ, וֶאֱמֶת יהוה לְעוֹלָם, הַלְלוּיָהּ.

הוֹדוּ לַיהוה כִּי טוֹב,   כִּי לְעוֹלָם חַסְדּוֹ.
יֹאמַר נָא יִשְׂרָאֵל, כִּי לְעוֹלָם חַסְדּוֹ.
יֹאמְרוּ נָא בֵית אַהֲרֹן,   כִּי לְעוֹלָם חַסְדּוֹ.
יֹאמְרוּ נָא יִרְאֵי יהוה,   כִּי לְעוֹלָם חַסְדּוֹ.

הַלְלוּ אֶת ה' כָּל גּוֹיִם — **Praise HASHEM, all you nations.**
Why should *non*-Jews praise God for His kindness to us?

There have been many times in our history when our enemies made secret plans to harm us — but God protected us. He spoiled their evil plans and helped us in ways that we did not even know about. For such miracles, our enemies should praise God, because they — not we — know how kind He was to us.

called out to God when I was in trouble and God answered by making me free. HASHEM is with me so I am not afraid — wnat can a person do to me? HASHEM is with me to help me, so I can face my enemies. It is better to seek HASHEM's protection than to trust the promises of people. It is better to seek HASHEM's protection than to trust the promises of princes. All the nations surround me, but I can defeat them by praying to HASHEM. They keep on surrounding me, but I can defeat them by praying to HASHEM. They surround me like bees, but they disappear like thorns burned by fire; I can defeat them by praying to HASHEM. They shove me to make me fall, but HASHEM helps me. God is my strength and I sing His praises, because He saved me. In the tents of righteous people there is a happy song about how HASHEM saves: "HASHEM's right hand does great things! HASHEM's right hand is raised high; HASHEM's right hand does great things!" I will not die — I will live and tell what HASHEM does! Even though God made me suffer, He did not let me die. Open for me the gates of the righteous *Bais Hamikdash;* I will enter through them and thank God. This is HASHEM's gate; righteous people enter through it. I thank You because You answered me; You were the One Who saved me. I thank You because You answered me; You were the One Who saved me. The stone that the builders scorn has become the cornerstone. The stone that the builders scorn has become the cornerstone. HASHEM made this happen — we think it is wonderful. HASHEM made this happen — we think it is wonderful. HASHEM made this great day — let us celebrate and be happy on it. HASHEM made this great day — let us celebrate and be happy on it.

O HASHEM, please save us!

O HASHEM, please save us!

O HASHEM, please make us successful!

O HASHEM, please make us successful!

lessed be everyone who comes to serve HASHEM — we bless you as the *Kohanim* used to bless visitors to the *Bais Hamikdash.* Blessed be everyone who comes to serve HASHEM — we bless you as the *Kohanim* used to bless visitors to the *Bais Hamikdash.*

מִן הַמֵּצַר קָרָאתִי יָּה, עָנָנִי בַמֶּרְחָב יָה. יהוה לִי לֹא אִירָא, מַה יַעֲשֶׂה לִי אָדָם. יהוה לִי בְּעֹזְרָי, וַאֲנִי אֶרְאֶה בְשֹׂנְאָי. טוֹב לַחֲסוֹת בַּיהוה, מִבְּטֹחַ בָּאָדָם. טוֹב לַחֲסוֹת בַּיהוה מִבְּטֹחַ בִּנְדִיבִים. כָּל גוֹיִם סְבָבוּנִי, בְּשֵׁם יהוה כִּי אֲמִילַם. סַבּוּנִי גַם סְבָבוּנִי, בְּשֵׁם יהוה כִּי אֲמִילַם. סַבּוּנִי כִדְבֹרִים דֹּעֲכוּ כְּאֵשׁ קוֹצִים, בְּשֵׁם יהוה כִּי אֲמִילַם. דָּחֹה דְחִיתַנִי לִנְפֹּל, וַיהוה עֲזָרָנִי. עָזִּי וְזִמְרָת יָהּ, וַיְהִי לִי לִישׁוּעָה. קוֹל רִנָּה וִישׁוּעָה בְּאָהֳלֵי צַדִּיקִים, יְמִין יהוה עֹשָׂה חָיִל. יְמִין יהוה רוֹמֵמָה, יְמִין יהוה עֹשָׂה חָיִל. לֹא אָמוּת כִּי אֶחְיֶה, וַאֲסַפֵּר מַעֲשֵׂי יָהּ. יַסֹּר יִסְּרַנִּי יָּהּ, וְלַמָּוֶת לֹא נְתָנָנִי. פִּתְחוּ לִי שַׁעֲרֵי צֶדֶק, אָבֹא בָם אוֹדֶה יָהּ. זֶה הַשַּׁעַר לַיהוה, צַדִּיקִים יָבֹאוּ בוֹ. אוֹדְךָ כִּי עֲנִיתָנִי, וַתְּהִי לִי לִישׁוּעָה. אוֹדְךָ כִּי עֲנִיתָנִי, וַתְּהִי לִי לִישׁוּעָה. אֶבֶן מָאֲסוּ הַבּוֹנִים, הָיְתָה לְרֹאשׁ פִּנָּה. אֶבֶן מָאֲסוּ הַבּוֹנִים, הָיְתָה לְרֹאשׁ פִּנָּה. מֵאֵת יהוה הָיְתָה זֹּאת, הִיא נִפְלָאת בְּעֵינֵינוּ. מֵאֵת יהוה הָיְתָה זֹּאת, הִיא נִפְלָאת בְּעֵינֵינוּ. זֶה הַיּוֹם עָשָׂה יהוה, נָגִילָה וְנִשְׂמְחָה בוֹ. זֶה הַיּוֹם עָשָׂה יהוה, נָגִילָה וְנִשְׂמְחָה בוֹ.

אָנָּא יהוה הוֹשִׁיעָה נָּא.

אָנָּא יהוה הוֹשִׁיעָה נָּא.

אָנָּא יהוה הַצְלִיחָה נָּא.

אָנָּא יהוה הַצְלִיחָה נָּא.

בָּרוּךְ הַבָּא בְּשֵׁם יהוה, בֵּרַכְנוּכֶם מִבֵּית יהוה. בָּרוּךְ הַבָּא בְּשֵׁם יהוה, בֵּרַכְנוּכֶם מִבֵּית יהוה. אֵל יהוה

HASHEM is the true God and He shows us the light — may we soon be able to tie our festival offerings and bring them up to the corners of the Altar. HASHEM is the true God and He shows us the light — may we soon be able to tie our festival offerings and bring them up to the corners of the Altar. You are my God and I will thank You; You are my God and I will say You are great. You are my God and I will thank You; You are my God and I will say You are great. Give thanks to HASHEM for He is good, His kindness lasts forever! Give thanks to HASHEM for He is good, His kindness lasts forever!

Everything that You made will praise You, HASHEM our God. Your most righteous people, who do what You want them to, and all of Your nation the Family of Israel with glad song will thank, bless, praise and proclaim You as the King in every way they can. It is good to thank You and it is right to praise You, because You are God forever.

וַיָּאֶר לָנוּ, אִסְרוּ חַג בַּעֲבֹתִים, עַד קַרְנוֹת הַמִּזְבֵּחַ. אֵל יהוה וַיָּאֶר לָנוּ, אִסְרוּ חַג בַּעֲבֹתִים, עַד קַרְנוֹת הַמִּזְבֵּחַ. אֵלִי אַתָּה וְאוֹדֶךָּ, אֱלֹהַי אֲרוֹמְמֶךָּ. אֵלִי אַתָּה וְאוֹדֶךָּ, אֱלֹהַי אֲרוֹמְמֶךָּ. הוֹדוּ לַיהוה כִּי טוֹב, כִּי לְעוֹלָם חַסְדּוֹ. הוֹדוּ לַיהוה כִּי טוֹב, כִּי לְעוֹלָם חַסְדּוֹ.

יְהַלְלוּךָ יהוה אֱלֹהֵינוּ כָּל מַעֲשֶׂיךָ, וַחֲסִידֶיךָ צַדִּיקִים עוֹשֵׂי רְצוֹנֶךָ, וְכָל עַמְּךָ בֵּית יִשְׂרָאֵל בְּרִנָּה יוֹדוּ וִיבָרְכוּ וִישַׁבְּחוּ וִיפָאֲרוּ וִירוֹמְמוּ וְיַעֲרִיצוּ וְיַקְדִּישׁוּ וְיַמְלִיכוּ אֶת שִׁמְךָ מַלְכֵּנוּ, כִּי לְךָ טוֹב לְהוֹדוֹת וּלְשִׁמְךָ נָאֶה לְזַמֵּר, כִּי מֵעוֹלָם וְעַד עוֹלָם אַתָּה אֵל.

Give thanks to HASHEM for He is good —
His kindness lasts forever!
Give thanks to the God of the angels —
His kindness lasts forever!
Give thanks to the Lord of lords —
His kindness lasts forever!
To Him Who does great miracles without
help— His kindness lasts forever!
To Him Who made the heavenly bodies with
understanding — His kindness lasts forever!
To Him Who spread dry land upon the
oceans — His kindness lasts forever!
To Him Who made the great lights in the sky —
his kindness lasts forever!
To Him Who made the sun to be the ruler
of the daytime — His kindness lasts forever!
To Him Who made the moon and stars
to be the rulers of the nighttime —
His kindness lasts forever!
To Him Who struck Egypt by killing their
firstborn — His kindness lasts forever!
To Him Who took the Jews out from among
the Egyptians — His kindness lasts forever!
With a strong hand and an outstretched
arm — His kindness lasts forever!
To Him Who divided the Sea of Reeds
into parts — His kindness lasts forever!
To Him Who led the Jews through it —
His kindness lasts forever!
To Him Who threw Pharaoh and his army
into the Sea of Reeds —
His kindness lasts forever!
To Him Who led His people through the
desert — His kindness lasts forever!
To Him Who struck down great kings —
His kindness lasts forever!
To Him Who killed strong kings —
His kindness lasts forever!
Sichon, the king of the Emorites —
His kindness lasts forever!
And Og, the king of Bashan —
His kindness lasts forever!
To Him Who gave their land to be ours
forever — His kindness lasts forever!
To belong forever to Israel, His servant —
His kindness lasts forever!
When we were lowly slaves He remembered
us — His kindness lasts forever!
And He saved us from our enemies —
His kindness lasts forever!
He gives food to all people —
His kindness lasts forever!
Give thanks to the God of heaven —
His kindness lasts forever!

הודו לַיהוה כִּי טוֹב, כִּי לְעוֹלָם חַסְדּוֹ.

הוֹדוּ לֵאלֹהֵי הָאֱלֹהִים, כִּי לְעוֹלָם חַסְדּוֹ.

הוֹדוּ לַאֲדֹנֵי הָאֲדֹנִים, כִּי לְעוֹלָם חַסְדּוֹ.

לְעֹשֵׂה נִפְלָאוֹת גְּדֹלוֹת לְבַדּוֹ, כִּי לְעוֹלָם חַסְדּוֹ.

לְעֹשֵׂה הַשָּׁמַיִם בִּתְבוּנָה, כִּי לְעוֹלָם חַסְדּוֹ.

לְרוֹקַע הָאָרֶץ עַל הַמָּיִם, כִּי לְעוֹלָם חַסְדּוֹ.

לְעֹשֵׂה אוֹרִים גְּדֹלִים, כִּי לְעוֹלָם חַסְדּוֹ.

אֶת הַשֶּׁמֶשׁ לְמֶמְשֶׁלֶת בַּיּוֹם, כִּי לְעוֹלָם חַסְדּוֹ.

אֶת הַיָּרֵחַ וְכוֹכָבִים
לְמֶמְשְׁלוֹת בַּלָּיְלָה, כִּי לְעוֹלָם חַסְדּוֹ.

לְמַכֵּה מִצְרַיִם בִּבְכוֹרֵיהֶם, כִּי לְעוֹלָם חַסְדּוֹ.

וַיּוֹצֵא יִשְׂרָאֵל מִתּוֹכָם, כִּי לְעוֹלָם חַסְדּוֹ.

בְּיָד חֲזָקָה וּבִזְרוֹעַ נְטוּיָה, כִּי לְעוֹלָם חַסְדּוֹ.

לְגֹזֵר יַם סוּף לִגְזָרִים, כִּי לְעוֹלָם חַסְדּוֹ.

וְהֶעֱבִיר יִשְׂרָאֵל בְּתוֹכוֹ, כִּי לְעוֹלָם חַסְדּוֹ.

וְנִעֵר פַּרְעֹה וְחֵילוֹ בְיַם סוּף, כִּי לְעוֹלָם חַסְדּוֹ.

לְמוֹלִיךְ עַמּוֹ בַּמִּדְבָּר, כִּי לְעוֹלָם חַסְדּוֹ.

לְמַכֵּה מְלָכִים גְּדֹלִים, כִּי לְעוֹלָם חַסְדּוֹ.

וַיַּהֲרֹג מְלָכִים אַדִּירִים, כִּי לְעוֹלָם חַסְדּוֹ.

לְסִיחוֹן מֶלֶךְ הָאֱמֹרִי, כִּי לְעוֹלָם חַסְדּוֹ.

וּלְעוֹג מֶלֶךְ הַבָּשָׁן, כִּי לְעוֹלָם חַסְדּוֹ.

וְנָתַן אַרְצָם לְנַחֲלָה, כִּי לְעוֹלָם חַסְדּוֹ.

נַחֲלָה לְיִשְׂרָאֵל עַבְדּוֹ, כִּי לְעוֹלָם חַסְדּוֹ.

שֶׁבְּשִׁפְלֵנוּ זָכַר לָנוּ, כִּי לְעוֹלָם חַסְדּוֹ.

וַיִּפְרְקֵנוּ מִצָּרֵינוּ, כִּי לְעוֹלָם חַסְדּוֹ.

נֹתֵן לֶחֶם לְכָל בָּשָׂר, כִּי לְעוֹלָם חַסְדּוֹ.

הוֹדוּ לְאֵל הַשָּׁמָיִם, כִּי לְעוֹלָם חַסְדּוֹ.

The soul of every living being will bless Your Name, HASHEM our God, and everyone's spirit will always give glory to Your memory, our King. You are God in This World and in the World to Come. Except for You we have no other King who can free and save us. You free us, rescue us, care for us, and show us mercy in every time of trouble and distress. We have no God except for You. You are the God of everything that happens, from beginning to end, the God of all living beings and Master of all generations. You are given many praises, You guide the world with kindness and the people with mercy. HASHEM neither slumbers nor sleeps. He wakes up sleepers, arouses slumberers, makes people able to speak, unties the ropes of prisoners, helps people rise after they fall, and straightens up the crippled. You are the only One we thank for all of this.

Even if our mouth were as flowing with songs as the sea flows with water, if our tongue could sing as many songs as the sea's waves, and if our lips could praise as much as the heaven is broad, if our eyes were as bright as the sun and the moon, if our hands were spread out like the eagles flying in the sky, and if our feet were as fast as deer — we still could not thank You enough, HASHEM our God, and the God of our ancestors. We could not bless Your Name enough for even one of the thousands and millions of favors that You did for our ancestors and for us. You saved us from Egypt, HASHEM our God, and freed us from slavery. In hunger You fed us, and in good times You supported us. You saved us from being killed by the sword or epidemics, and You let us avoid long and painful illness. Until now Your mercy has helped us and Your kindness never left us. HASHEM our God — please do not ever abandon us!

Therefore, the parts of our body that You put into us, the soul and spirit You breathed into our noses, and the tongues You put into our mouth — they will all thank, bless, and praise You, and call out that only You are the King. Every mouth will thank You, every tongue will swear to obey You, every knee will bend to You, every back will

נִשְׁמַת כָּל חַי תְּבָרֵךְ אֶת שִׁמְךָ יהוה אֱלֹהֵינוּ, וְרוּחַ כָּל בָּשָׂר תְּפָאֵר וּתְרוֹמֵם זִכְרְךָ מַלְכֵּנוּ תָּמִיד. מִן הָעוֹלָם וְעַד הָעוֹלָם אַתָּה אֵל, וּמִבַּלְעָדֶיךָ אֵין לָנוּ מֶלֶךְ גּוֹאֵל וּמוֹשִׁיעַ. פּוֹדֶה וּמַצִּיל וּמְפַרְנֵס וּמְרַחֵם בְּכָל עֵת צָרָה וְצוּקָה, אֵין לָנוּ מֶלֶךְ אֶלָּא אָתָּה. אֱלֹהֵי הָרִאשׁוֹנִים וְהָאַחֲרוֹנִים, אֱלוֹהַּ כָּל בְּרִיּוֹת, אֲדוֹן כָּל תּוֹלָדוֹת, הַמְהֻלָּל בְּרֹב הַתִּשְׁבָּחוֹת, הַמְנַהֵג עוֹלָמוֹ בְּחֶסֶד וּבְרִיּוֹתָיו בְּרַחֲמִים. וַיהוה לֹא יָנוּם וְלֹא יִישָׁן. הַמְעוֹרֵר יְשֵׁנִים, וְהַמֵּקִיץ נִרְדָּמִים, וְהַמֵּשִׂיחַ אִלְּמִים, וְהַמַּתִּיר אֲסוּרִים, וְהַסּוֹמֵךְ נוֹפְלִים, וְהַזּוֹקֵף כְּפוּפִים. לְךָ לְבַדְּךָ אֲנַחְנוּ מוֹדִים.

אִלּוּ פִינוּ מָלֵא שִׁירָה כַּיָּם, וּלְשׁוֹנֵנוּ רִנָּה כַּהֲמוֹן גַּלָּיו, וְשִׂפְתוֹתֵינוּ שֶׁבַח כְּמֶרְחֲבֵי רָקִיעַ, וְעֵינֵינוּ מְאִירוֹת כַּשֶּׁמֶשׁ וְכַיָּרֵחַ, וְיָדֵינוּ פְרוּשׂוֹת כְּנִשְׁרֵי שָׁמָיִם, וְרַגְלֵינוּ קַלּוֹת כָּאַיָּלוֹת, אֵין אֲנַחְנוּ מַסְפִּיקִים לְהוֹדוֹת לְךָ, יהוה אֱלֹהֵינוּ וֵאלֹהֵי אֲבוֹתֵינוּ, וּלְבָרֵךְ אֶת שְׁמֶךָ, עַל אַחַת מֵאֶלֶף אֶלֶף אַלְפֵי אֲלָפִים וְרִבֵּי רְבָבוֹת פְּעָמִים הַטּוֹבוֹת שֶׁעָשִׂיתָ עִם אֲבוֹתֵינוּ וְעִמָּנוּ. מִמִּצְרַיִם גְּאַלְתָּנוּ יהוה אֱלֹהֵינוּ, וּמִבֵּית עֲבָדִים פְּדִיתָנוּ, בְּרָעָב זַנְתָּנוּ, וּבְשָׂבָע כִּלְכַּלְתָּנוּ, מֵחֶרֶב הִצַּלְתָּנוּ, וּמִדֶּבֶר מִלַּטְתָּנוּ, וּמֵחֳלָיִם רָעִים וְנֶאֱמָנִים דִּלִּיתָנוּ. עַד הֵנָּה עֲזָרוּנוּ רַחֲמֶיךָ, וְלֹא עֲזָבוּנוּ חֲסָדֶיךָ. וְאַל תִּטְּשֵׁנוּ יהוה אֱלֹהֵינוּ לָנֶצַח.

עַל כֵּן, אֵבָרִים שֶׁפִּלַּגְתָּ בָּנוּ, וְרוּחַ וּנְשָׁמָה שֶׁנָּפַחְתָּ בְּאַפֵּינוּ, וְלָשׁוֹן אֲשֶׁר שַׂמְתָּ בְּפִינוּ, הֵן הֵם יוֹדוּ וִיבָרְכוּ וִישַׁבְּחוּ וִיפָאֲרוּ וִירוֹמְמוּ וְיַעֲרִיצוּ וְיַקְדִּישׁוּ וְיַמְלִיכוּ אֶת שִׁמְךָ מַלְכֵּנוּ. כִּי כָל פֶּה לְךָ יוֹדֶה, וְכָל לָשׁוֹן לְךָ תִשָּׁבַע, וְכָל בֶּרֶךְ לְךָ תִכְרַע, וְכָל קוֹמָה לְפָנֶיךָ

bow to You, all hearts will fear You, and people will sing to You with their most sincere feelings. As the Torah says: "All my bones will say, 'HASHEM, who is like You?' You save the poor person from someone stronger than he, and You save the poor and needy person from a robber."

Who is like You? Who is equal to You? Who can be compared to You? You are the great, strong and awesome God, Who created heaven and earth. We praise, glorify, and bless Your holy Name, as King David said, "Bless HASHEM, O my soul, and let me bless His Holy Name sincerely!"

 God — You are so strong, the glory of Your Name is so great, You are mighty forever and people are in awe by You because of Your awesome deeds. O King, You sit on a very high throne.

 e lives forever and His Name is high and holy. As Scripture writes, "O righteous people, sing happily before HASHEM; it is right for good people to praise Him." The mouth of good people will praise You; the words of righteous people will bless You; the tongue of deeply religious people will glorify You; the sincerity of holy people will declare that You are holy.

 henever large numbers of Your Jewish people get together, Your Name will be glorified with happy song, our King. It is everyone's duty, HASHEM our God and the God of our forefathers, to thank, praise, glorify, bless, and sing to You — even more than all the songs and praises of David son of Jesse, Your servant, Your anointed King.

תִּשְׁתַּחֲוֶה, וְכָל לְבָבוֹת יִירָאוּךָ, וְכָל קֶרֶב וּכְלָיוֹת יְזַמְּרוּ לִשְׁמֶךָ, כַּדָּבָר שֶׁכָּתוּב: כָּל עַצְמֹתַי תֹּאמַרְנָה, יהוה מִי כָמוֹךָ. מַצִּיל עָנִי מֵחָזָק מִמֶּנּוּ, וְעָנִי וְאֶבְיוֹן מִגֹּזְלוֹ.

מִי יִדְמֶה לָּךְ, וּמִי יִשְׁוֶה לָּךְ, וּמִי יַעֲרֹךְ לָךְ. הָאֵל הַגָּדוֹל הַגִּבּוֹר וְהַנּוֹרָא, אֵל עֶלְיוֹן קֹנֵה שָׁמַיִם וָאָרֶץ. נְהַלֶּלְךָ וּנְשַׁבֵּחֲךָ וּנְפָאֶרְךָ וּנְבָרֵךְ אֶת שֵׁם קָדְשֶׁךָ, כָּאָמוּר: לְדָוִד, בָּרְכִי נַפְשִׁי אֶת יהוה, וְכָל קְרָבַי אֶת שֵׁם קָדְשׁוֹ.

הָאֵל בְּתַעֲצֻמוֹת עֻזֶּךָ, הַגָּדוֹל בִּכְבוֹד שְׁמֶךָ, הַגִּבּוֹר לָנֶצַח וְהַנּוֹרָא בְּנוֹרְאוֹתֶיךָ, הַמֶּלֶךְ הַיּוֹשֵׁב עַל כִּסֵּא רָם וְנִשָּׂא.

שׁוֹכֵן עַד מָרוֹם וְקָדוֹשׁ שְׁמוֹ. וְכָתוּב: רַנְּנוּ צַדִּיקִים בַּיהוה, לַיְשָׁרִים נָאוָה תְהִלָּה. בְּפִי יְשָׁרִים תִּתְהַלָּל, וּבְדִבְרֵי צַדִּיקִים תִּתְבָּרַךְ, וּבִלְשׁוֹן חֲסִידִים תִּתְרוֹמָם, וּבְקֶרֶב קְדוֹשִׁים תִּתְקַדָּשׁ.

וּבְמַקְהֲלוֹת רִבְבוֹת עַמְּךָ בֵּית יִשְׂרָאֵל, בְּרִנָּה יִתְפָּאֵר שִׁמְךָ מַלְכֵּנוּ בְּכָל דּוֹר וָדוֹר. שֶׁכֵּן חוֹבַת כָּל הַיְצוּרִים, לְפָנֶיךָ יהוה אֱלֹהֵינוּ וֵאלֹהֵי אֲבוֹתֵינוּ, לְהוֹדוֹת לְהַלֵּל לְשַׁבֵּחַ לְפָאֵר לְרוֹמֵם לְהַדֵּר לְבָרֵךְ לְעַלֵּה וּלְקַלֵּס, עַל כָּל דִּבְרֵי שִׁירוֹת וְתִשְׁבָּחוֹת דָּוִד בֶּן יִשַׁי עַבְדְּךָ מְשִׁיחֶךָ.

שׁוֹכֵן עַד — **He lives forever.**

Even though God lives forever and His holiness is so great, He wants to be served and praised by ordinary people like us. He gave the Torah to us because He wants everyone to do His *mitzvos*.

In the next sentence we say that God is praised and blessed by good, righteous, religious, and holy people. But what of just simple, ordinary Jews? Does He even want *us* to praise Him? Yes! As the next paragraph states: God is happy to be thanked and blessed "whenever large numbers of Jewish people get together."

May Your Name be praised forever in heaven and on earth, our King, God, the great and holy King. HASHEM our God and the God of our forefathers, it is right that people give You song and praises, power, authority, victory, greatness, strength, praise, glory, holiness, kingship, blessings and thanks-givings — now and forever. We bless You HASHEM, God, King Who is declared to be great through our praises, God Whom we give thanks, the Master of wonders, Who chooses our songs of praise — King, God, Who gives life to the world.

יִשְׁתַּבַּח שִׁמְךָ לָעַד מַלְכֵּנוּ, הָאֵל הַמֶּלֶךְ הַגָּדוֹל וְהַקָּדוֹשׁ בַּשָּׁמַיִם וּבָאָרֶץ. כִּי לְךָ נָאֶה יהוה אֱלֹהֵינוּ וֵאלֹהֵי אֲבוֹתֵינוּ, שִׁיר וּשְׁבָחָה, הַלֵּל וְזִמְרָה, עֹז וּמֶמְשָׁלָה, נֶצַח גְּדֻלָּה וּגְבוּרָה, תְּהִלָּה וְתִפְאֶרֶת, קְדֻשָּׁה וּמַלְכוּת, בְּרָכוֹת וְהוֹדָאוֹת מֵעַתָּה וְעַד עוֹלָם. בָּרוּךְ אַתָּה יהוה, אֵל מֶלֶךְ גָּדוֹל בַּתִּשְׁבָּחוֹת, אֵל הַהוֹדָאוֹת, אֲדוֹן הַנִּפְלָאוֹת, הַבּוֹחֵר בְּשִׁירֵי זִמְרָה, מֶלֶךְ אֵל חֵי הָעוֹלָמִים.

Raise the cup and recite the blessing:

We bless You, HASHEM our God, King of the whole world, Who creates the fruit of the grapevine.

בָּרוּךְ אַתָּה יהוה אֱלֹהֵינוּ מֶלֶךְ הָעוֹלָם, בּוֹרֵא פְּרִי הַגָּפֶן.

After drinking the fourth cup of wine, recite the following blessing.
[On the Sabbath add the words in brackets.]

We bless You, HASHEM our God, King of the whole world, for the grapevine and the fruit of the grapevine, for the fruits of the field and for the pleasant, good, and broad land that You were pleased to let our ancestors inherit, to eat its fruits and enjoy its goodness. HASHEM our God, have mercy on Israel, Your nation; on Jerusalem, Your city; on the Temple Mount, the resting place of Your honor; on Your Altar; and on Your *Bais Hamikdash*. Rebuild Jerusalem, Your holy city, quickly in our lifetime; bring us there, let us rejoice in its rebuilding, eat its fruit, and be satisfied with its goodness. We will bless You for it in holiness and purity. [And may it please You to make us healthy on this Shabbos day.] Make us happy on this Festival of Matzos, for You, HASHEM, are good and You do good for everyone; so we thank You for the land and the fruit of the grapevine. We bless You, HASHEM, for the Land and for the fruit of the grapevine.

בָּרוּךְ אַתָּה יהוה אֱלֹהֵינוּ מֶלֶךְ הָעוֹלָם, עַל הַגֶּפֶן וְעַל פְּרִי הַגֶּפֶן, וְעַל תְּנוּבַת הַשָּׂדֶה, וְעַל אֶרֶץ חֶמְדָּה טוֹבָה וּרְחָבָה, שֶׁרָצִיתָ וְהִנְחַלְתָּ לַאֲבוֹתֵינוּ, לֶאֱכֹל מִפִּרְיָהּ וְלִשְׂבֹּעַ מִטּוּבָהּ. רַחֵם יהוה אֱלֹהֵינוּ עַל יִשְׂרָאֵל עַמֶּךָ, וְעַל יְרוּשָׁלַיִם עִירֶךָ, וְעַל צִיּוֹן מִשְׁכַּן כְּבוֹדֶךָ, וְעַל מִזְבְּחֶךָ, וְעַל הֵיכָלֶךָ. וּבְנֵה יְרוּשָׁלַיִם עִיר הַקֹּדֶשׁ בִּמְהֵרָה בְיָמֵינוּ, וְהַעֲלֵנוּ לְתוֹכָהּ, וְשַׂמְּחֵנוּ בְּבִנְיָנָהּ, וְנֹאכַל מִפִּרְיָהּ, וְנִשְׂבַּע מִטּוּבָהּ, וּנְבָרֶכְךָ עָלֶיהָ בִּקְדֻשָּׁה וּבְטָהֳרָה. [וּרְצֵה וְהַחֲלִיצֵנוּ בְּיוֹם הַשַּׁבָּת הַזֶּה] וְשַׂמְּחֵנוּ בְּיוֹם חַג הַמַּצּוֹת הַזֶּה. כִּי אַתָּה יהוה טוֹב וּמֵטִיב לַכֹּל, וְנוֹדֶה לְךָ עַל הָאָרֶץ וְעַל פְּרִי הַגֶּפֶן. בָּרוּךְ אַתָּה יהוה, עַל הָאָרֶץ וְעַל פְּרִי הַגֶּפֶן.

נִרְצָה

NIRTZAH

he *Seder* is now ending according to its law, according to all its rules and regulations. Just as we have had the honor of making the *Seder,* so may we deserve to bring the real *Pesach* offering.

O pure God Who lives in heaven, please bring back the honor of the congregation of Jews, which You said would be too many to count. May You soon guide us, we who are the fruits of Your Jewish vine, and bring us free, to Jerusalem, with a happy song.

Next year in Jerusalem!

חֲסַל סִדּוּר פֶּסַח כְּהִלְכָתוֹ, כְּכָל מִשְׁפָּטוֹ וְחֻקָתוֹ, כַּאֲשֶׁר זָכִינוּ לְסַדֵּר אוֹתוֹ, כֵּן נִזְכֶּה לַעֲשׂוֹתוֹ.

זָךְ שׁוֹכֵן מְעוֹנָה, קוֹמֵם קְהַל עֲדַת מִי מָנָה, בְּקָרוֹב נַהֵל נִטְעֵי כַנָּה, פְּדוּיִם לְצִיּוֹן בְּרִנָּה.

לְשָׁנָה הַבָּאָה בִּירוּשָׁלָיִם.

חֲסַל סִדּוּר פֶּסַח — The *Seder* is now ending.
A Jew's highest goal is to serve God and be able to do His *mitzvos*. By the time the *Seder* is over, we have worked very hard: cleaning our homes, preparing Pesach food, and carrying out the laws of the *Seder*. How should God reward us? By bringing *Mashiach* and allowing us to bring the *Korban Pesach* in Jerusalem.

On the first night, recite the following:

And it happened at midnight.

וּבְכֵן וַיְהִי בַּחֲצִי הַלַּיְלָה:

You performed many miracles at night.	אָז רוֹב נִסִּים הִפְלֵאתָ בַּלַּיְלָה.
These miracles came at the beginning of a "watch" [the night is divided into four "watches"] of this night.	בְּרֹאשׁ אַשְׁמוֹרֶת זֶה הַלַּיְלָה.
You helped Abraham the righteous convert defeat the four kings in the middle of the night	גֵּר צֶדֶק נִצַּחְתּוֹ כְּנֶחֱלַק לוֹ לַיְלָה.
— and it happened at midnight.	וַיְהִי בַּחֲצִי הַלַּיְלָה.
You judged King Abimelech of Gerar in a dream at night	דַּנְתָּ מֶלֶךְ גְּרָר בַּחֲלוֹם הַלַּיְלָה.
You frightened Laban the Aramean in the darkness of the night	הִפְחַדְתָּ אֲרַמִּי בְּאֶמֶשׁ לַיְלָה.
Jacob fought against an angel and overcame him at night	וַיָּשַׂר יִשְׂרָאֵל לְמַלְאָךְ וַיּוּכַל לוֹ לַיְלָה.
— and it happened at midnight.	וַיְהִי בַּחֲצִי הַלַּיְלָה.
The firstborn of Egypt were destroyed at midnight.	זֶרַע בְּכוֹרֵי פַתְרוֹס מָחַצְתָּ בַּחֲצִי הַלַּיְלָה.
The Egyptians could not find their treasures when they arose that night.	חֵילָם לֹא מָצְאוּ בְּקוּמָם בַּלַּיְלָה.
You used the stars to battle against the army of Sisera, the ruler of Charoshes, at night	טִיסַת נְגִיד חֲרוֹשֶׁת סִלִּיתָ בְּכוֹכְבֵי לַיְלָה.
— and it happened at midnight.	וַיְהִי בַּחֲצִי הַלַּיְלָה.
Sancherib planned to raise his hand against Jerusalem but You caused his army to fall dead, at night.	יָעַץ מְחָרֵף לְנוֹפֵף אִוּוּי הוֹבַשְׁתָּ פְגָרָיו בַּלַּיְלָה.
Those who worshiped the Babylonian idol Baal, You humbled at night.	כָּרַע בֵּל וּמַצָּבוֹ בְּאִישׁוֹן לַיְלָה.
To Daniel, the man of delights, you taught the secret of the dream that Nevuchadnezzar dreamt at night	לְאִישׁ חֲמוּדוֹת נִגְלָה רָז חֲזוֹת לַיְלָה.
— and it happened at midnight.	וַיְהִי בַּחֲצִי הַלַּיְלָה.
Belshazzar, who drank from the holy vessels of the Bais Hamikdash, was killed at night	מִשְׁתַּכֵּר בִּכְלֵי קֹדֶשׁ נֶהֱרַג בּוֹ בַּלַּיְלָה.
Daniel, who was saved from the lions' den, interpreted the frightening dreams of the night.	נוֹשַׁע מִבּוֹר אֲרָיוֹת פּוֹתֵר בִּעֲתוּתֵי לַיְלָה.
Haman, the Aggagite, who hated the Jews, wrote letters against them at night	שִׂנְאָה נָטַר אֲגָגִי וְכָתַב סְפָרִים בַּלַּיְלָה.
— and it happened at midnight.	וַיְהִי בַּחֲצִי הַלַּיְלָה.
You began Your victory over Haman by not allowing Ahasuerus to sleep at night.	עוֹרַרְתָּ נִצְחֲךָ עָלָיו בְּנֶדֶד שְׁנַת לַיְלָה.
May God answer: "Tread on the evil nations," to the guardian angel of Israel who asks, "What will be the outcome of this long exile night?"	פּוּרָה תִדְרוֹךְ לְשׁוֹמֵר מַה מִלַּיְלָה.
When Mashiach comes, God will command the light of day to shine for the righteous, but the wicked will be surrounded by the darkness of the night	צָרַח כַּשּׁוֹמֵר וְשָׂח אָתָא בֹקֶר וְגַם לַיְלָה.
— and it happened at midnight.	וַיְהִי בַּחֲצִי הַלַּיְלָה.
Hasten the time of Mashiach when there will be only day and no night.	קָרֵב יוֹם אֲשֶׁר הוּא לֹא יוֹם וְלֹא לַיְלָה.
God, let it be known that Yours is the day and Yours is the night.	רָם הוֹדַע כִּי לְךָ הַיּוֹם אַף לְךָ הַלַּיְלָה.
Appoint guards to stand around Your city, Jerusalem, all the day and all the night.	שׁוֹמְרִים הַפְקֵד לְעִירְךָ כָּל הַיּוֹם וְכָל הַלַּיְלָה.
Let the brilliance of the day brighten the darkness of the night	תָּאִיר כְּאוֹר יוֹם חֶשְׁכַת לַיְלָה.
— and it happened at midnight.	וַיְהִי בַּחֲצִי הַלַּיְלָה.

וּבְכֵן וַיְהִי בַּחֲצִי הַלַּיְלָה — **And it happened at midnight.**

The final plague in Egypt — the Plague of the Firstborn — happened at midnight, and God told Moses that every year the night of Pesach would be a time when we would be protected. This song follows the Aleph-Beis as it gives a long list of other miracles that took place at night.

On the second night recite the following:

And you shall say, "This is the feast of Pesach."

 וּבְכֵן וַאֲמַרְתֶּם זֶבַח פֶּסַח:

You have shown Your mighty powers	on Pesach.	בְּפֶסַח. אֹמֶץ גְּבוּרוֹתֶיךָ הִפְלֵאתָ
By making it the first of all Festivals, You honored	Pesach.	פֶּסַח. בְּרֹאשׁ כָּל מוֹעֲדוֹת נִשֵּׂאתָ
You revealed to Abraham what would happen in Egypt at midnight	on Pesach	פֶּסַח. גִּלִּיתָ לְאֶזְרָחִי חֲצוֹת לֵיל
— and you shall say, "This is the feast of Pesach."		וַאֲמַרְתֶּם זֶבַח פֶּסַח.
You knocked on Abraham's door to visit him in the heat of the day,	on Pesach.	בְּפֶסַח. דְּלָתָיו דָּפַקְתָּ כְּחֹם הַיּוֹם
Abraham fed the angels matzos	on Pesach.	בְּפֶסַח. הִסְעִיד נוֹצְצִים עֻגוֹת מַצּוֹת
Abraham ran to the cattle — a reminder of the bull for the future *Chagigah* offering	of Pesach	פֶּסַח. וְאֶל הַבָּקָר רָץ זֵכֶר לְשׁוֹר עֵרֶךְ
— and you shall say, "This is the feast of Pesach."		וַאֲמַרְתֶּם זֶבַח פֶּסַח.
The people of Sodom angered God and were burnt by fire	on Pesach.	בְּפֶסַח. זֹעֲמוּ סְדוֹמִים וְלוֹהֲטוּ בָּאֵשׁ
Lot separated himself from the people of Sodom, and he baked matzos	on Pesach.	פֶּסַח. חֻלַּץ לוֹט מֵהֶם וּמַצּוֹת אָפָה בְּקֵץ
You destroyed the Egyptian cities of Moph and Noph, as You passed through them	on Pesach	בְּפֶסַח. טֵאטֵאתָ אַדְמַת מֹף וְנֹף בְּעָבְרְךָ
— and you shall say, "This is the feast of Pesach."		וַאֲמַרְתֶּם זֶבַח פֶּסַח.
God, You destroyed the Egyptian firstborn and You protected the Jews on the night	of Pesach.	פֶּסַח. יָהּ רֹאשׁ כָּל אוֹן מָחַצְתָּ בְּלֵיל שִׁמּוּר
You passed over the homes of the Jews on whose doors was the blood of	the Pesach.	פֶּסַח. כַּבִּיר עַל בֵּן בְּכוֹר פָּסַחְתָּ בְּדַם
You didn't let the Angel of Death enter Jewish homes	on Pesach	בְּפֶסַח. לְבִלְתִּי תֵּת מַשְׁחִית לָבֹא בִּפְתָחַי
— and you shall say, "This is the feast of Pesach."		וַאֲמַרְתֶּם זֶבַח פֶּסַח.
Jericho, the fortified and sealed city, was conquered during the time	of Pesach.	פֶּסַח. מְסֻגֶּרֶת סֻגָּרָה בְּעִתּוֹתֵי
Midian was destroyed because of the merit of the *Omer*, which was offered	on Pesach.	פֶּסַח. נִשְׁמְדָה מִדְיָן בִּצְלִיל שְׂעוֹרֵי עֹמֶר
The Assyrian heroes Pul and Lud were consumed by the fire of an angel	on Pesach	פֶּסַח. שֹׂרְפוּ מִשְׁמַנֵּי פּוּל וְלוּד בִּיקַד יְקוֹד
— and you shall say, "This is the feast of Pesach."		וַאֲמַרְתֶּם זֶבַח פֶּסַח.
"Today we will be in Nob, and tomorrow we will conquer Jerusalem," said Sancherib, and he waited until the arrival	of Pesach.	פֶּסַח. עוֹד הַיּוֹם בְּנֹב לַעֲמוֹד עַד גָּעָה עוֹנַת
A hand wrote on the wall, telling Belshazzar about the destruction of Babylonia	on Pesach.	בְּפֶסַח. פַּס יַד כָּתְבָה לְקַעֲקֵעַ צוּל
Belshazzar's watchman looked for an enemy attack as the king arranged his table	on Pesach	בְּפֶסַח. צָפֹה הַצָּפִית עָרוֹךְ הַשֻּׁלְחָן
— and you shall say, "This is the feast of Pesach."		וַאֲמַרְתֶּם זֶבַח פֶּסַח.
Esther gathered the Jews to fast for three days	on Pesach.	בְּפֶסַח. קָהָל כִּנְּסָה הֲדַסָּה צוֹם לְשַׁלֵּשׁ
The wicked Haman was killed and hanged on a fifty-cubit gallows	on Pesach.	בְּפֶסַח. רֹאשׁ מִבֵּית רָשָׁע מָחַצְתָּ בְּעֵץ חֲמִשִּׁים
May You bring a double misfortune upon the nation of Edom	on Pesach.	בְּפֶסַח. שְׁתֵּי אֵלֶּה רֶגַע תָּבִיא לְעוּצִית
May You again show Your strength as You did on the night when You sanctified	Pesach	פֶּסַח. תָּעֹז יָדְךָ וְתָרוּם יְמִינְךָ כְּלֵיל הִתְקַדֵּשׁ חַג
— and you shall say, "This is the feast of Pesach."		וַאֲמַרְתֶּם זֶבַח פֶּסַח.

וּבְכֵן וַאֲמַרְתֶּם זֶבַח פֶּסַח — **And you shall say, "This is the feast of Pesach."**
Throughout Jewish history — even before we went down into Egypt — many important miracles and other events happened on Pesach. This song tells about them in *Aleph-Beis* order.

57 / YOUTH HAGGADAH

On both nights continue here.

To Him praise is due!
To Him praise is fitting!

כִּי לוֹ נָאֶה, כִּי לוֹ יָאֶה:

owerful in kingship, perfectly distinguished, His groups of angels say to him: "To You and only to You; to You, yes, to You; to You, surely to You; to You, Hashem, belongs the Kingship." To Him praise is due. To Him praise is fitting.

אַדִּיר בִּמְלוּכָה, בָּחוּר כַּהֲלָכָה, גְּדוּדָיו יֹאמְרוּ לוֹ, לְךָ וּלְךָ, לְךָ כִּי לְךָ, לְךָ אַף לְךָ, לְךָ יהוה הַמַּמְלָכָה, כִּי לוֹ נָאֶה, כִּי לוֹ יָאֶה.

Supreme in kingship, perfectly glorious, His faithful people say to Him: "To You and only to You; to You, yes, to You; to You, surely to You; to You, Hashem, belongs the kingship." To Him praise is due. To Him praise is fitting.

דָּגוּל בִּמְלוּכָה, הָדוּר כַּהֲלָכָה, וָתִיקָיו יֹאמְרוּ לוֹ, לְךָ וּלְךָ, לְךָ כִּי לְךָ, לְךָ אַף לְךָ, לְךָ יהוה הַמַּמְלָכָה, כִּי לוֹ נָאֶה, כִּי לוֹ יָאֶה.

Worthy in kingship, perfectly mighty, His angels say unto Him: "To You and only to You; to You, yes, to You; to You, surely to You; to You, Hashem, is the kingship." To Him praise is due. To Him praise is fitting.

זַכַּאי בִּמְלוּכָה, חָסִין כַּהֲלָכָה, טַפְסְרָיו יֹאמְרוּ לוֹ, לְךָ וּלְךָ, לְךָ כִּי לְךָ, לְךָ אַף לְךָ, לְךָ יהוה הַמַּמְלָכָה, כִּי לוֹ נָאֶה, כִּי לוֹ יָאֶה.

Alone in kingship, perfectly all-powerful, His scholars say to Him: "To You and only to You; to You, yes, to You; to You, surely to You; to You, Hashem, is the kingship." To Him praise is due. To Him praise is fitting.

יָחִיד בִּמְלוּכָה, כַּבִּיר כַּהֲלָכָה, לִמּוּדָיו יֹאמְרוּ לוֹ, לְךָ וּלְךָ, לְךָ כִּי לְךָ, לְךָ אַף לְךָ, לְךָ יהוה הַמַּמְלָכָה, כִּי לוֹ נָאֶה, כִּי לוֹ יָאֶה.

Ruling in kingship, perfectly wondrous, His surrounding angels say to Him: "To You and only to You; to You, yes, to You; to You, surely to You; to You, Hashem, is the kingship." To Him praise is due. To Him praise is fitting.

מוֹשֵׁל בִּמְלוּכָה, נוֹרָא כַּהֲלָכָה, סְבִיבָיו יֹאמְרוּ לוֹ, לְךָ וּלְךָ, לְךָ כִּי לְךָ, לְךָ אַף לְךָ, לְךָ יהוה הַמַּמְלָכָה, כִּי לוֹ נָאֶה, כִּי לוֹ יָאֶה.

Humble in Kingship, perfectly the Redeemer, His righteous people say to Him: "To You and only to You; to You, yes, to You; to You, surely to You; to You, Hashem, is the kingship." To Him praise is due. To Him praise is fitting.

עָנָיו בִּמְלוּכָה, פּוֹדֶה כַּהֲלָכָה, צַדִּיקָיו יֹאמְרוּ לוֹ, לְךָ וּלְךָ, לְךָ כִּי לְךָ, לְךָ אַף לְךָ, לְךָ יהוה הַמַּמְלָכָה, כִּי לוֹ נָאֶה, כִּי לוֹ יָאֶה.

Holy in kingship, perfectly merciful, His troops of angels say to Him: "To You and only to You; to You, yes, to You; to You, surely to You; to You, Hashem, is the kingship." To Him praise is due. To Him praise is fitting.

קָדוֹשׁ בִּמְלוּכָה, רַחוּם כַּהֲלָכָה, שִׁנְאַנָּיו יֹאמְרוּ לוֹ, לְךָ וּלְךָ, לְךָ כִּי לְךָ, לְךָ אַף לְךָ, לְךָ יהוה הַמַּמְלָכָה, כִּי לוֹ נָאֶה, כִּי לוֹ יָאֶה.

Mighty in kingship, perfectly supporting, His perfect people say to Him: "To You and only to You; to You, yes, to You; to You, surely to You; to You, Hashem, is the kingship." To Him praise is due. To Him praise is fitting.

תַּקִּיף בִּמְלוּכָה, תּוֹמֵךְ כַּהֲלָכָה, תְּמִימָיו יֹאמְרוּ לוֹ, לְךָ וּלְךָ, לְךָ כִּי לְךָ, לְךָ אַף לְךָ, לְךָ יהוה הַמַּמְלָכָה, כִּי לוֹ נָאֶה, כִּי לוֹ יָאֶה.

כִּי לוֹ נָאֶה — To Him praise is due!
No one understands God's greatness better than the angels and the *tzaddikim*. This song follows the *Aleph-Beis* to describe God's greatness, and to tell how the angels and *tzaddikim* praise Him.

אַדִּיר הוּא — He is Mighty.
This song uses the twenty-two letters of the *Aleph-Beis* to describe God's attributes. The repeated theme of this song is a prayer for the rebuilding of the *Bais Hamikdash* soon, during our lifetime.

He is mighty. May He soon rebuild His House, speedily, yes speedily, in our days, soon. God, rebuild; God, rebuild; rebuild Your House soon!

He is excellent. He is great. He is elevated. May He soon rebuild His House, speedily, yes speedily, in our days, soon. God, rebuild; God, rebuild; rebuild Your House soon!

He is glorious. He is true. He is worthy. He is righteous. May He soon rebuild His House, speedily, yes speedily, in our days, soon. God, rebuild; God, rebuild; rebuild Your House soon!

He is pure. He is special. He is grand. He is learned. He is King. He is awesome. He is strong. He is all-powerful. He redeems. He is all-righteous. May He soon rebuild His House, speedily, yes speedily, in our days, soon. God, rebuild; God, rebuild; rebuild Your House soon!

He is holy. He is merciful. He is the Almighty. He is powerful. May He soon rebuild His House, speedily, yes speedily, in our days, soon. God, rebuild; God, rebuild; rebuild Your House soon!

אַדִּיר הוּא. יִבְנֶה בֵיתוֹ בְּקָרוֹב, בִּמְהֵרָה, בִּמְהֵרָה, בְּיָמֵינוּ בְּקָרוֹב. אֵל בְּנֵה, אֵל בְּנֵה, בְּנֵה בֵיתְךָ בְּקָרוֹב.

בָּחוּר הוּא. גָּדוֹל הוּא. דָּגוּל הוּא. יִבְנֶה בֵיתוֹ בְּקָרוֹב, בִּמְהֵרָה, בִּמְהֵרָה, בְּיָמֵינוּ בְּקָרוֹב. אֵל בְּנֵה, אֵל בְּנֵה, בְּנֵה בֵיתְךָ בְּקָרוֹב.

הָדוּר הוּא. וָתִיק הוּא. זַכַּאי הוּא. חָסִיד הוּא. יִבְנֶה בֵיתוֹ בְּקָרוֹב, בִּמְהֵרָה, בִּמְהֵרָה, בְּיָמֵינוּ בְּקָרוֹב. אֵל בְּנֵה, אֵל בְּנֵה, בְּנֵה בֵיתְךָ בְּקָרוֹב.

טָהוֹר הוּא. יָחִיד הוּא. כַּבִּיר הוּא. לָמוּד הוּא. מֶלֶךְ הוּא. נוֹרָא הוּא. סַגִּיב הוּא. עִזּוּז הוּא. פּוֹדֶה הוּא. צַדִּיק הוּא. יִבְנֶה בֵיתוֹ בְּקָרוֹב, בִּמְהֵרָה, בִּמְהֵרָה, בְּיָמֵינוּ בְּקָרוֹב. אֵל בְּנֵה, אֵל בְּנֵה, בְּנֵה בֵיתְךָ בְּקָרוֹב.

קָדוֹשׁ הוּא. רַחוּם הוּא. שַׁדַּי הוּא. תַּקִּיף הוּא. יִבְנֶה בֵיתוֹ בְּקָרוֹב, בִּמְהֵרָה, בִּמְהֵרָה, בְּיָמֵינוּ בְּקָרוֹב. אֵל בְּנֵה, אֵל בְּנֵה, בְּנֵה בֵיתְךָ בְּקָרוֹב.

ho knows one? I know one! One is our God, in heaven and on earth.

Who knows two? I know two! Two are the Tablets of the Ten Commandments; One is our God, in heaven and on earth.

Who knows three? I know three! Three are the Fathers [of the Jewish nation — Abraham, Isaac and Jacob]; two are the Tablets of the Ten Commandments; One is our God, in heaven and on earth.

Who knows four? I know four! Four are the Mothers [of the Jewish nation — Sarah, Rebecca, Rachel and Leah]; three are the Fathers; two are the Tablets of the Ten Commandments; One is our God, in heaven and on earth.

Who knows five? I know five! Five are the books of Torah [*Bereishis, Sh'mos, Vayikra, Bamidbar, Devarim*]; four are the Mothers; three are the Fathers; two are the Tablets of the Ten Commandments; One is our God, in heaven and on earth.

Who know six? I know six! Six are the portions of the Mishnah [*Zeraim, Moed, Nashim, Nezikin, Kodashim, Toharos*]; five are the books of Torah; four are the Mothers; three are the Fathers; two are the Tablets of the Ten Commandments; One is our God, in heaven and on earth.

Who knows seven? I know seven! Seven are the days of the week; six are the portions of the Mishnah; five are the books of the Torah; four are the Mothers; three are the Fathers; two are the Tablets of the Ten Commandments; One is our God, in heaven and on earth.

Who knows eight? I know eight! Eight are the days before circumcision; seven are the days of the week; six are the portions of the Mishnah; five are the books of Torah; four are the Mothers; three are the Fathers; two are the Tablets of the Ten Commandments; One is our God, in heaven and on the earth.

אֶחָד מִי יוֹדֵעַ?

אֶחָד אֲנִי יוֹדֵעַ. אֶחָד אֱלֹהֵינוּ שֶׁבַּשָּׁמַיִם וּבָאָרֶץ.

שְׁנַיִם מִי יוֹדֵעַ? שְׁנַיִם אֲנִי יוֹדֵעַ. שְׁנֵי לֻחוֹת הַבְּרִית, אֶחָד אֱלֹהֵינוּ שֶׁבַּשָּׁמַיִם וּבָאָרֶץ.

שְׁלֹשָׁה מִי יוֹדֵעַ? שְׁלֹשָׁה אֲנִי יוֹדֵעַ. שְׁלֹשָׁה אָבוֹת, שְׁנֵי לֻחוֹת הַבְּרִית, אֶחָד אֱלֹהֵינוּ שֶׁבַּשָּׁמַיִם וּבָאָרֶץ.

אַרְבַּע מִי יוֹדֵעַ? אַרְבַּע אֲנִי יוֹדֵעַ. אַרְבַּע אִמָּהוֹת, שְׁלֹשָׁה אָבוֹת, שְׁנֵי לֻחוֹת הַבְּרִית, אֶחָד אֱלֹהֵינוּ שֶׁבַּשָּׁמַיִם וּבָאָרֶץ.

חֲמִשָּׁה מִי יוֹדֵעַ? חֲמִשָּׁה אֲנִי יוֹדֵעַ. חֲמִשָּׁה חֻמְשֵׁי תוֹרָה, אַרְבַּע אִמָּהוֹת, שְׁלֹשָׁה אָבוֹת, שְׁנֵי לֻחוֹת הַבְּרִית, אֶחָד אֱלֹהֵינוּ שֶׁבַּשָּׁמַיִם וּבָאָרֶץ.

שִׁשָּׁה מִי יוֹדֵעַ? שִׁשָּׁה אֲנִי יוֹדֵעַ. שִׁשָּׁה סִדְרֵי מִשְׁנָה, חֲמִשָּׁה חֻמְשֵׁי תוֹרָה, אַרְבַּע אִמָּהוֹת, שְׁלֹשָׁה אָבוֹת, שְׁנֵי לֻחוֹת הַבְּרִית, אֶחָד אֱלֹהֵינוּ שֶׁבַּשָּׁמַיִם וּבָאָרֶץ.

שִׁבְעָה מִי יוֹדֵעַ? שִׁבְעָה אֲנִי יוֹדֵעַ. שִׁבְעָה יְמֵי שַׁבַּתָּא, שִׁשָּׁה סִדְרֵי מִשְׁנָה, חֲמִשָּׁה חֻמְשֵׁי תוֹרָה, אַרְבַּע אִמָּהוֹת, שְׁלֹשָׁה אָבוֹת, שְׁנֵי לֻחוֹת הַבְּרִית, אֶחָד אֱלֹהֵינוּ שֶׁבַּשָּׁמַיִם וּבָאָרֶץ.

שְׁמוֹנָה מִי יוֹדֵעַ? שְׁמוֹנָה אֲנִי יוֹדֵעַ. שְׁמוֹנָה יְמֵי מִילָה, שִׁבְעָה יְמֵי שַׁבַּתָּא, שִׁשָּׁה סִדְרֵי מִשְׁנָה, חֲמִשָּׁה חֻמְשֵׁי תוֹרָה, אַרְבַּע אִמָּהוֹת, שְׁלֹשָׁה אָבוֹת, שְׁנֵי לֻחוֹת הַבְּרִית, אֶחָד אֱלֹהֵינוּ שֶׁבַּשָּׁמַיִם וּבָאָרֶץ.

Who knows nine? I know nine! Nine are the months of pregnancy; eight are the days before circumcision; seven are the days of the week; six are the portions of the Mishnah; five are the books of the Torah; four are the Mothers; three are the Fathers; two are the Tablets of the Ten Commandments; One is our God, in heaven and on the earth.

Who knows ten? I know ten! Ten are the Ten Commandments; nine are the months of pregnancy; eight are the days before circumcision; seven are the days of the week; six are the portions of the Mishnah; five are the books of the Torah; four are the Mothers; three are the Fathers; two are the Tablets of the Ten Commandments; One is our God, in heaven and on earth.

Who knows eleven? I know eleven! Eleven are the stars [in Joseph's dream]; ten are the Ten Commandments; nine are the months of pregnancy; eight are the days before circumcision; seven are the days of the week; six are the portions of the Mishnah; five are the books of the Torah; four are the Mothers; three are the Fathers; two are the Tablets of the Ten Commandments; One is our God, in heaven and on earth.

Who knows twelve? I know twelve! Twelve are the tribes [Jacob's sons]; eleven are the stars; ten are the Ten Commandments; nine are the months of pregnancy; eight are the days before circumcision; seven are the days of the week; six are the portions of the Mishnah; five are the books of the Torah; four are the Mothers; three are the Fathers; two are the Tablets of the Ten Commandments; One is our God, in heaven and on earth.

Who knows thirteen? I know thirteen! Thirteen are God's Ways of Mercy; twelve are the tribes; eleven are the stars; ten are the Ten Commandments; nine are the months of pregnancy; eight are the days before circumcision; seven are the days of the week; six are the portions of the Mishnah; five are the books of the Torah; four are the Mothers; three are the Fathers; two are the Tablets of the Ten Commandments; One is our God, in heaven and on earth.

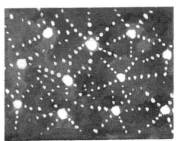

תִּשְׁעָה מִי יוֹדֵעַ? תִּשְׁעָה אֲנִי יוֹדֵעַ. תִּשְׁעָה יַרְחֵי לֵדָה, שְׁמוֹנָה יְמֵי מִילָה, שִׁבְעָה יְמֵי שַׁבַּתָּא, שִׁשָּׁה סִדְרֵי מִשְׁנָה, חֲמִשָּׁה חֻמְשֵׁי תוֹרָה, אַרְבַּע אִמָּהוֹת, שְׁלֹשָׁה אָבוֹת, שְׁנֵי לֻחוֹת הַבְּרִית, אֶחָד אֱלֹהֵינוּ שֶׁבַּשָּׁמַיִם וּבָאָרֶץ.

עֲשָׂרָה מִי יוֹדֵעַ? עֲשָׂרָה אֲנִי יוֹדֵעַ. עֲשָׂרָה דִבְּרַיָּא, תִּשְׁעָה יַרְחֵי לֵדָה, שְׁמוֹנָה יְמֵי מִילָה, שִׁבְעָה יְמֵי שַׁבַּתָּא, שִׁשָּׁה סִדְרֵי מִשְׁנָה, חֲמִשָּׁה חֻמְשֵׁי תוֹרָה, אַרְבַּע אִמָּהוֹת, שְׁלֹשָׁה אָבוֹת, שְׁנֵי לֻחוֹת הַבְּרִית, אֶחָד אֱלֹהֵינוּ שֶׁבַּשָּׁמַיִם וּבָאָרֶץ.

אַחַד עָשָׂר מִי יוֹדֵעַ? אַחַד עָשָׂר אֲנִי יוֹדֵעַ. אַחַד עָשָׂר כּוֹכְבַיָּא, עֲשָׂרָה דִבְּרַיָּא, תִּשְׁעָה יַרְחֵי לֵדָה, שְׁמוֹנָה יְמֵי מִילָה, שִׁבְעָה יְמֵי שַׁבַּתָּא, שִׁשָּׁה סִדְרֵי מִשְׁנָה, חֲמִשָּׁה חֻמְשֵׁי תוֹרָה, אַרְבַּע אִמָּהוֹת, שְׁלֹשָׁה אָבוֹת, שְׁנֵי לֻחוֹת הַבְּרִית, אֶחָד אֱלֹהֵינוּ שֶׁבַּשָּׁמַיִם וּבָאָרֶץ.

שְׁנֵים עָשָׂר מִי יוֹדֵעַ? שְׁנֵים עָשָׂר אֲנִי יוֹדֵעַ. שְׁנֵים עָשָׂר שִׁבְטַיָּא, אַחַד עָשָׂר כּוֹכְבַיָּא, עֲשָׂרָה דִבְּרַיָּא, תִּשְׁעָה יַרְחֵי לֵדָה, שְׁמוֹנָה יְמֵי מִילָה, שִׁבְעָה יְמֵי שַׁבַּתָּא, שִׁשָּׁה סִדְרֵי מִשְׁנָה, חֲמִשָּׁה חֻמְשֵׁי תוֹרָה, אַרְבַּע אִמָּהוֹת, שְׁלֹשָׁה אָבוֹת, שְׁנֵי לֻחוֹת הַבְּרִית, אֶחָד אֱלֹהֵינוּ שֶׁבַּשָּׁמַיִם וּבָאָרֶץ.

שְׁלֹשָׁה עָשָׂר מִי יוֹדֵעַ? שְׁלֹשָׁה עָשָׂר אֲנִי יוֹדֵעַ. שְׁלֹשָׁה עָשָׂר מִדַּיָּא, שְׁנֵים עָשָׂר שִׁבְטַיָּא, אַחַד עָשָׂר כּוֹכְבַיָּא, עֲשָׂרָה דִבְּרַיָּא, תִּשְׁעָה יַרְחֵי לֵדָה, שְׁמוֹנָה יְמֵי מִילָה, שִׁבְעָה יְמֵי שַׁבַּתָּא, שִׁשָּׁה סִדְרֵי מִשְׁנָה, חֲמִשָּׁה חֻמְשֵׁי תוֹרָה, אַרְבַּע אִמָּהוֹת, שְׁלֹשָׁה אָבוֹת, שְׁנֵי לֻחוֹת הַבְּרִית, אֶחָד אֱלֹהֵינוּ שֶׁבַּשָּׁמַיִם וּבָאָרֶץ.

ne **Kid,** one kid, that Father bought for two zuzim, one kid, one kid.

A **cat** then came and ate the kid, that Father bought for two zuzim, one kid, one kid.

A **dog** then came and bit the cat, that ate the kid, that Father bought for two zuzim, one kid, one kid.

A **stick** then came and hit the dog, that bit the cat, that ate the kid, that Father bought for two zuzim, one kid, one kid.

A **fire** then came and burned the stick, that hit the dog, that bit the cat, that ate the kid, that Father bought for two zuzim, one kid, one kid.

Water then came and drowned the fire, that burned the stick, that hit the dog, that bit

חַד גַּדְיָא, חַד גַּדְיָא, דְּזַבִּין אַבָּא בִּתְרֵי זוּזֵי, חַד גַּדְיָא חַד גַּדְיָא.

וְאָתָא שׁוּנְרָא וְאָכְלָה לְגַדְיָא, דְּזַבִּין אַבָּא בִּתְרֵי זוּזֵי, חַד גַּדְיָא חַד גַּדְיָא.

וְאָתָא כַלְבָּא וְנָשַׁךְ לְשׁוּנְרָא, דְּאָכְלָא לְגַדְיָא, דְּזַבִּין אַבָּא בִּתְרֵי זוּזֵי, חַד גַּדְיָא חַד גַּדְיָא.

וְאָתָא חוּטְרָא וְהִכָּה לְכַלְבָּא, דְּנָשַׁךְ לְשׁוּנְרָא, דְּאָכְלָה לְגַדְיָא, דְּזַבִּין אַבָּא בִּתְרֵי זוּזֵי, חַד גַּדְיָא חַד גַּדְיָא.

וְאָתָא נוּרָא וְשָׂרַף לְחוּטְרָא, דְּהִכָּה לְכַלְבָּא, דְּנָשַׁךְ לְשׁוּנְרָא, דְּאָכְלָה לְגַדְיָא, דְּזַבִּין אַבָּא בִּתְרֵי זוּזֵי, חַד גַּדְיָא חַד גַּדְיָא.

וְאָתָא מַיָּא וְכָבָה לְנוּרָא, דְּשָׂרַף לְחוּטְרָא, דְּהִכָּה לְכַלְבָּא, דְּנָשַׁךְ לְשׁוּנְרָא,

the cat, that ate the kid, that Father bought for two zuzim, one kid, one kid.

An **ox** then came and drank the water, that drowned the fire, that burned the stick, that hit the dog, that bit the cat, that ate the kid, that Father bought for two zuzim, one kid, one kid.

The **slaughterer** then came and slaughtered the ox, that drank the water, that drowned the fire, that burned the stick, that hit the dog, that bit the cat, that ate the kid, that Father bought for two zuzim, one kid, one kid.

The **Angel of Death** then came and killed the slaughterer, who slaughtered the ox, that drank the water, that drowned the fire, that burned the stick, that hit the dog, that bit the cat, that ate the kid, that Father bought for two zuzim, one kid, one kid.

דְּאָכְלָה לְגַדְיָא, דְּזַבִּין אַבָּא בִּתְרֵי זוּזֵי, חַד גַּדְיָא חַד גַּדְיָא.

וְאָתָא **תוֹרָא** וְשָׁתָה לְמַיָּא, דְּכָבָה לְנוּרָא, דְּשָׂרַף לְחוּטְרָא, דְּהִכָּה לְכַלְבָּא, דְּנָשַׁךְ לְשׁוּנְרָא, דְּאָכְלָה לְגַדְיָא, דְּזַבִּין אַבָּא בִּתְרֵי זוּזֵי, חַד גַּדְיָא חַד גַּדְיָא.

וְאָתָא **הַשּׁוֹחֵט** וְשָׁחַט לְתוֹרָא, דְּשָׁתָא לְמַיָּא, דְּכָבָה לְנוּרָא, דְּשָׂרַף לְחוּטְרָא, דְּהִכָּה לְכַלְבָּא, דְּנָשַׁךְ לְשׁוּנְרָא, דְּאָכְלָה לְגַדְיָא, דְּזַבִּין אַבָּא בִּתְרֵי זוּזֵי, חַד גַּדְיָא חַד גַּדְיָא.

וְאָתָא **מַלְאַךְ הַמָּוֶת** וְשָׁחַט לְשׁוֹחֵט, דְּשָׁחַט לְתוֹרָא, דְּשָׁתָה לְמַיָּא, דְּכָבָה לְנוּרָא, דְּשָׂרַף לְחוּטְרָא, דְּהִכָּה לְכַלְבָּא, דְּנָשַׁךְ לְשׁוּנְרָא, דְּאָכְלָה לְגַדְיָא, דְּזַבִּין אַבָּא בִּתְרֵי זוּזֵי, חַד גַּדְיָא חַד גַּדְיָא.

God Himself then came and slew the Angel of Death, who killed the slaughterer, who slaughtered the ox, that drank the water, that drowned the fire, that burned the stick, that hit the dog, that bit the cat, that ate the kid, that Father bought for two zuzim, one kid, one kid.

וְאָתָא הַקָּדוֹשׁ בָּרוּךְ הוּא וְשָׁחַט לְמַלְאַךְ הַמָּוֶת, דְּשָׁחַט לְשׁוֹחֵט, דְּשָׁחַט לְתוֹרָא, דְּשָׁתָה לְמַיָּא, דְּכָבָה לְנוּרָא, דְּשָׂרַף לְחוּטְרָא, דְּהִכָּה לְכַלְבָּא, דְּנָשַׁךְ לְשׁוּנְרָא, דְּאָכְלָה לְגַדְיָא, דְּזַבִּין אַבָּא בִּתְרֵי זוּזֵי, חַד גַּדְיָא חַד גַּדְיָא.

חַד גַּדְיָא חַד גַּדְיָא — One kid, one kid

Many people have wondered why our rabbis decided to end the *Seder* with *Chad Gadya* [One Kid], which is so much like children's songs of other languages. The simple, cheerful words of this song must have a deeper meaning that makes it belong in the *Seder*. Indeed, many commentators have explained *Chad Gadya* in different ways. This is how the Vilna Gaon understood the song:

Isaac was ready to give his blessings to the wicked Esau. Instead, Jacob received the blessings after he had served his father the meat of two young goats. So it is as if he bought the blessings with the two baby goats.

חַד גַּדְיָא ... בִּתְרֵי זוּזֵי — One kid ... two zuzim.
The two *zuzim* stand for the two goats that Jacob served his father. Those goats were symbols for the *Pesach* offering and the *Chagigah* offering that Jacob's children would bring every Pesach.
The kid of the song stands for the blessings that Jacob received.
Of all Jacob's twelve sons, he considered Joseph to be the finest, so Jacob gave him the blessings and also passed the honor of being the firstborn to Joseph.

שׁוּנְרָא — A cat.
A cat stands for "jealousy." Joseph's brothers were jealous of him. They sold him into slavery, and because of that, the whole family later came to Egypt.

כַּלְבָּא — A dog.
Pharaoh is compared to a dog. The Egyptian "dog" did terrible things to the Jewish "cat."

חוּטְרָא — A stick.
God gave Moses a miraculous stick that he was to use to perform all the miracles. So that stick came to punish the Egyptian "dog."
Before he died, Moses gave his stick to Joshua. The stick was passed down through the generations. Even the miracles that took place in the *Bais Hamikdash* happened because of that holy stick.

נוּרָא — A fire.
The *Yetzer Hara* [Evil Inclination] is like a fire burning inside people. Because of that fire, our forefathers committed so many sins that the First *Bais Hamikdash* was burned down.

מַיָּא — Water.
The אַנְשֵׁי כְּנֶסֶת הַגְּדוֹלָה, *Men of the Great Assembly*, were the leaders of the Jewish nation during the early years of the Second *Bais Hamikdash*. They prayed to God that the Jewish people should never again have a *Yetzer Hara* to serve idols. These great men also established many laws to prevent Israel from sinning. They were like the water that puts out a fire.

תּוֹרָא — An ox.
The Romans were like a wild, strong ox. When the Jews once again began to turn away from God's service, He allowed the Romans to come to power. They destroyed the Second *Bais Hamikdash* and murdered countless Jews.

הַשּׁוֹחֵט — The slaughterer.
When the time comes to save the Jewish people from exile, God will send מָשִׁיחַ בֶּן יוֹסֵף, a *Mashiach from the tribe of Joseph*. He will fight against the enemies of our people, and begin to slaughter them.

מַלְאַךְ הַמָּוֶת — The Angel of Death.
Before the *Mashiach* from Joseph can win a complete victory, he will be killed in battle.

הַקָּדוֹשׁ בָּרוּךְ הוּא — God Himself.
At the end, God Himself will finish the task of saving us. When that happens we will once again have all the blessings that Jacob received from Isaac. That is why we keep repeating the whole chain of events, all the way back to, "One kid, one kid, that Father [Jacob] bought for two zuzim."